General editor: Graham Handley MA PH D

Brodie's Notes on William Shakespeare's
# Twelfth Night

Graham Handley   MA PH D
Formerly Principal Lecturer in English, College of All Saints, Tottenham

D1269950

**Pan Books** London, Sydney, and Auckland

First published 1985 by Pan Books Ltd,
Cavaye Place, London SW10 9PG
19 18 17 16 15
© Pan Books Ltd, 1985
ISBN 0 330 50191 7
Photoset by Parker Typesetting Service, Leicester
Printed and bound in Great Britain by
Richard Clay Ltd, Bungay, Suffolk

Other titles by Graham Handley in the Brodie's Notes series:
Macbeth
As You Like It
Much Ado About Nothing

# Contents

References in these Notes are to the
Arden Shakespeare: *Twelfth Night*,
but the Notes may be used with
any edition of the play.

# Preface

This student revision aid is based on the principle that in any close examination of Shakespeare's plays 'the text's the thing'. Seeing a performance, or listening to a tape or record of a performance, is essential and is in itself a valuable and stimulating experience in understanding and appreciation. However, a real evaluation of Shakespeare's greatness, of his universality and of the nature of his literary and dramatic art, can only be achieved by constant application to the texts of the plays themselves. These revised editions of Brodie's Notes are intended to supplement that process through detailed critical commentary.

The first aim of each book is to fix the whole play in the reader's mind by providing a concise summary of the plot, relating it back, where appropriate, to its source or sources. Subsequently the book provides a summary of each scene, followed by *critical comments*. These may convey its importance in the dramatic structure of the play, creation of atmosphere, indication of character development, significance of figurative language etc, and they will also explain or paraphrase difficult words or phrases and identify meaningful references. At the end of each act revision questions are set to test the student's specific and broad understanding and appreciation of the play.

An extended critical commentary follows this scene by scene analysis. This embraces such major elements as characterization, imagery, the use of blank verse and prose, soliloquies and other aspects of the play which the editor considers need close attention. The paramount aim is to send the reader back to the text. The book concludes with a series of revision questions which require a detailed knowledge of the play; the first of these has notes by the editor of what *might* be included in a written answer. The intention is to stimulate and to guide; the whole emphasis of this commentary is to encourage the student's *involvement* in the play, to develop disciplined critical responses and thus promote personal enrichment through the imaginative experience of our greatest writer.

Graham Handley

# Shakespeare and the Elizabethan playhouse

William Shakespeare was born in Stratford-upon-Avon in 1564, and there are reasons to suppose that he came from a relatively prosperous family. He was probably educated at Stratford Grammar School and, at the age of eighteen, married Anne Hathaway, who was twenty-six. They had three children, a girl born shortly after their marriage, followed by twins in 1585 (the boy died in 1596). It seems likely that Shakespeare left for London shortly after a company of visiting players had visited Stratford in 1585, for by 1592 – according to the jealous testimony of one of his fellow-writers Robert Greene – he was certainly making his way both as actor and dramatist. The theatres were closed because of the plague in 1593; when they reopened Shakespeare worked with the Lord Chamberlain's men, later the King's men, and became a shareholder in each of the two theatres with which he was most closely associated, the Globe and the Blackfriars. He later purchased New Place, a considerable property in his home town of Stratford, to which he retired in 1611; there he entertained his great contemporary Ben Jonson (1572–1637) and the poet Michael Drayton (1563–1631). An astute businessman, Shakespeare lived comfortably in the town until his death in 1616.

This is a very brief outline of the life of our greatest writer, for little more can be said of him with certainty, though the plays – and poems – are living witness to the wisdom, humanity and many-faceted nature of the man. He was both popular and successful as a dramatist, perhaps less so as an actor. He probably began work as a dramatist in the late 1580s, by collaborating with other playwrights and adapting old plays, and by 1598 Francis Meres was paying tribute to his excellence in both comedy and tragedy. His first original play was probably *Love's Labour's Lost* (1590) and while the theatres were closed during the plague he wrote his narrative poems *Venus and Adonis* (1593) and *The Rape of Lucrece* (1594). The sonnets were almost certainly written in the 1590s, though not published until 1609; the first 126 are addressed to a young man who was his friend and patron, while the rest are concerned with the 'dark lady'.

The dating of Shakespeare's plays has exercised scholars ever since the publication of the First Folio (1623), which listed them as comedies, histories and tragedies. It seems more important to look at them chronologically as far as possible, in order to trace Shakespeare's considerable development as a dramatist. The first period, say to the middle of the 1590s, included such plays as *Love's Labour's Lost*, *The Comedy of Errors*, *Richard III*, *The Taming of the Shrew*, *Romeo and Juliet* and *Richard II*. These early plays embrace the categories listed in the First Folio, so that Shakespeare the craftsman is evident in his capacity for variety of subject and treatment. The next phase includes *A Midsummer's Night's Dream*, *The Merchant of Venice*, *Henry IV Parts 1 and 2*, *Henry V* and *Much Ado About Nothing*, as well as *Julius Caesar*, *As You Like It* and *Twelfth Night*. These are followed, in the early years of the century, by his great tragic period: *Hamlet*, *Othello*, *King Lear* and *Macbeth*, with *Antony and Cleopatra* and *Coriolanus* belonging to 1607–09. The final phase embraces the romances (1610–13), *Cymbeline*, *The Tempest* and *The Winter's Tale* and the historical play *Henry VIII*.

Each of these revision aids will place the individual text under examination in the chronology of the remarkable dramatic output that spanned twenty years from the early 1590s to about 1613. The practical theatre for which Shakespeare wrote and acted derived from the inn courtyards in which performances had taken place, the few playhouses in his day being modelled on their structure. They were circular or hexagonal in shape, allowing the balconies and boxes around the walls full view of the stage. This large stage, which had no scenery, jutted out into the pit, the most extensive part of the theatre where the poorer people – the 'groundlings' – stood. There was no roof (though the Blackfriars, used from 1608 onwards, was an indoor theatre) and thus bad weather meant no performance. Certain plays were acted at court, and these private performances normally marked some special occasion. Costumes, often rich ones, were used, and music was a common feature, with musicians on or under the stage; this sometimes had additional features, for example a trapdoor to facilitate the entry of a ghost. Women were barred by law from appearing on stage, and all female parts were played by boy actors; this undoubtedly explains the many instances in Shakespeare where a woman has to conceal her identity by disguising

herself as a man, e.g. Rosalind in *As You Like It*, Viola in *Twelfth Night*.

Shakespeare and his contemporaries often adapted their plays from sources in history and literature, extending an incident or a myth or creating a dramatic narrative from known facts. They were always aware of their own audiences, and frequently included topical references, sometimes of a satirical flavour, which would appeal to – and be understood by – the ground lings as well as their wealthier patrons who occupied the boxes Shakespeare obviously learned much from his fellow dramatists and actors, being on good terms with many of them. Ben Jonson paid generous tribute to him in the lines prefaced to the First Folio of Shakespeare's plays:

Thou art a monument without a tomb,
And art alive still, while thy book doth live
And we have wits to read, and praise to give.

Among his contemporaries were Thomas Kyd (1558–94) and Christopher Marlowe (1564–93). Kyd wrote *The Spanish Tragedy*, the revenge motif here foreshadowing the much more sophisticated treatment evident in *Hamlet*, while Marlowe evolved the 'mighty line' of blank verse, a combination of natural speech and elevated poetry. The quality and variety of Shakespeare's blank verse owes something to the innovatory brilliance of Marlowe, but carries the stamp of individuality, richness of association, technical virtuosity and, above all, the genius of imaginative power.

The texts of Shakespeare's plays are still rich sources for scholars, and the editors of these revision aids have used the Arden editions of Shakespeare, which are regarded as pre-eminent for their scholarly approach. They are strongly recommended for advanced students, but other editions, like The New Penguin Shakespeare, The New Swan, The Signet are all good annotated editions currently available. A reading list of selected reliable works on the play being studied is provided at the end of each commentary and students are advised to turn to these as their interest in the play deepens.

# Literary terms used in these notes

In the *Scene summaries, commentaries, textual notes* and, particularly, in the sub-headings under *Style*, literary terms are used and defined (see the section on *Dramatic irony*, for example). Consequently only a few are listed here.

**Alliteration** Words close together in a phrase or line which begin with the same letter ('shrill and sound', 'four or five' and 'whoe'er I woo, myself would be his wife' (all from Act I, Scene 4).

**Simile** A comparison involving the use of 'like' or 'as' ('thy small pipe/Is as the maiden's organ' in Act I, Scene 4)and 'And like the haggard, check at every feather' in Act III, Scene 1).

**Metaphor** A compressed comparison *without* the use of 'like' or 'as' ('the north of my lady's opinion' in Act III, Scene 2) and 'Have you not set mine honour at the stake,/And baited it with all th' unmuzzled thoughts . . .' of Act III, Scene 1, where the metaphor is taken from bear-baiting, a contemporary Elizabethan sport.

**Pun** A word that has two or more meanings but which is pronounced or spelled the same. It is a feature of Shakespeare's comedy generally, and particularly prevalent in *Twelfth Night* (see 'hart' Act I Scene 1, 'Perchance', Act I Scene 2, 'tall' Act I Scene 3, for example).

# The play
## Plot, sources, treatment and date

### Plot

The twins Sebastian and Viola are shipwrecked on the coast of
Illyria; Viola thinks that her brother has been drowned and,
disguising herself as a page and dressing in clothes similar to
those worn by Sebastian, she adopts the name of Cesario and
enters the service of Orsino, Duke of Illyria. Meanwhile, unbeknown to her, her brother Sebastian has been saved by a sea
captain, Antonio, who becomes very attached to him.

Viola as 'Cesario' quickly makes herself essential to Duke
Orsino, who is in love with Olivia, a neighbouring heiress. Olivia,
in mourning for the death of her brother, will not listen to
Orsino's proposals; Orsino sends Viola as Cesario to woo Olivia
on his (Orsino's) behalf. Matters become complicated when
Olivia falls in love with 'Cesario'/Viola, who herself has fallen in
love with Orsino.

Meanwhile Olivia's household steward, Malvolio, has ant-
agonized the members of the household and Olivia's uncle, Sir
Toby Belch, by his overbearing manner and Puritanical
attitudes. Sir Toby (who has brought a foolish knight Sir
Andrew Aguecheek to woo Olivia), is always becoming drunk
and noisy; he falls foul of Malvolio. Maria, Olivia's maid, hatches
a conspiracy against Malvolio by writing a letter, purporting to
come from Olivia, which encourages Malvolio to love her and to
think that she is in love with him. Olivia is persuaded that
Malvolio is mad, and Maria and Sir Toby and the Clown (Feste)
keep him in a dark room.

Sir Andrew is being systematically swindled by Sir Toby, is
persuaded by him and by Fabian to challenge Cesario/Viola to a
duel – Sir Andrew being jealous of Cesario's success with Olivia.
Cesario and Sir Andrew face each other in fear and trembling,
each having been given fearsome accounts of the other's
(non-existent) ability as a fencer. The duel is unexpectedly
broken up by Antonio – who had saved Sebastian – and who
now, seeing the duellists, mistakes Cesario/Viola for Sebastian.
He had loaned Sebastian his purse, and now asks 'Cesario' for

help; 'Cesario' is bewildered, and Antonio is arrested by Orsino's officers for an old offence against Illyria in a sea fight. He of course cannot understand why Viola does not acknowledge him, but he names Sebastian, so that Viola now believes that her brother is alive.

Next Sir Toby, Sir Andrew and Fabian encounter Sebastian, (they of course think it is Cesario/Viola) and begin fighting with him; this is broken up by Olivia, who persuades Sebastian to become betrothed to her. Meanwhile, Malvolio is tormented by the Clown as 'Sir Topas', and the fact of mistaken identity is not resolved until the final coming together of all the characters. Olivia marries Sebastian and, when the latter is seen on stage with Viola, everything is explained. Brother and sister are reunited, Viola is to marry the Duke, Sir Toby has already married Maria, and Malvolio vows revenge on everybody for the trick that has been played on him. Fittingly, Feste has the last word – in a song.

## Sources

Kenneth Muir, in his *The Sources of Shakespeare's Plays* (1977) brilliantly traces the playwright's use of his own plays as part sources for *Twelfth Night*, instancing the mistaken identity of the twins in *The Comedy of Errors*, and the girl as page who acts as go-between for the man she is in love with and the women *he* is in love with in *The Two Gentlemen of Verona*. Here we shall concentrate on the distant and then the more immediate sources of *Twelfth Night*.

In *Gl'Inganni*, an Italian play (1592), the disguised girl is called Cesare; in another play of the same name by another playwright, published thirty years earlier, the girl is in love with her master, a direct anticipation of Viola's situation with Orsino. The first play of this name, (L'Inganni) and much earlier in time (1538), seems to have a direct connection with *Twelfth Night*, since its disguises and situations anticipate those of the later play. Here the heroine disguises herself as a man, enters the service of a man whose mistress she had been, and is sent by him as a messenger to the woman he now loves. That woman; like Olivia in *Twelfth Night*, falls in love with the messenger. Her brother later appears and, as in *Twelfth Night*, is mistaken for her and becomes the lady's lover. The heroine ultimately marries her master. The main parallels with *Twelfth Night* are striking.

Unquestionably the main source for *Twelfth Night* is Barnabe Riche's *Riche his Farewell to Militarie Profession* (1581), which contains the imprisonment of a wife for madness 'in a darke house' and mentions in its dedication a number of dances and terms used by Shakespeare in Act I Scene 3, the joking of Sir Toby with Sir Andrew. The main story concerns Apolonius and Silla; the latter falls in love with her father's guest Apolonius and follows him on his departure. She survives an attempted rape and then a shipwreck, disguises herself as a man and takes the name of her twin brother Silvio. She finds Apolonius, enters his service, and is used by him as a messenger to Julina whom he loves. Julina herself falls in love with the messenger and counsels 'his' silence. The complications are compounded by the arrival of the real Silvio, who meets Julina by accident (compare this with Sebastian's meeting with Olivia) and is invited to supper, later sharing her bed. She becomes pregnant, rejects Apolonius who, learning that 'Silvio' (really Silla) is her favoured one, imprisons Silla and threatens to kill her if she does not marry Julina. Silla has to reveal that she is a woman, whereupon Apolonius marries her and Silvio, learning of their marriage, returns to wed Julina.

## Treatment

The differences in *Twelfth Night* will be obvious, and we do not intend to explore them in depth here. Since it is a romantic comedy, the lustful sea captain and the attempted rape in Riche would have been inappropriate, as would the sleeping together of Olivia and Sebastian, who are merely betrothed before a later celebration. The 'mad' note in Riche is expanded into a sick/comic sub-plot. Olivia's house and the activities of Sir Toby, the Clown, Fabian and Sir Andrew as well as that plot pivot Maria, all smack of contemporary Elizabethan life and derive from the immediate source of Shakespeare's own imagination. Moreover. Riche's Constantinople becomes more conveniently and vaguely Illyria, appropriately romantic in court and house for the unravelling of the mistaken identities.

# Date

The date of *Twelfth Night* has exercised scholars over the last 300 years, and one writer, Leslie Hotson, devoted a whole book to *The First Night of 'Twelfth Night'*. The evidence for a date of composition and performance some time in 1600–01 is incontrovertible, and that evidence is both internal and external. Firstly, there is the entry in Manningham's Diary for 1601 (correctly 1602) in which he refers to 'Twelfth Night or what you will', comparing it to *The Comedy of Errors*. He describes how 'the steward believes his Lady Widow was in love with him by counterfeiting a letter as from his lady . . . prescribing his gesture in smiling . . . they took him to be mad'. (We have modernized Manningham's spelling). This is of course the Malvolio plot. Manningham's entry refers to a performance at the Middle Temple, but this was not necessarily the first performance.

On 6 January 1601 the Queen entertained a Don Orsino, Duke of Bracciano, to music and festivities on the traditional 'twelfth night' after Christmas, but it seems doubtful (despite Hotson's research) that the play could have been performed then. The coincidence of the name 'Orsino' is a striking one, and since the young nobleman made such a good impression on his visit Shakespeare may have used it in the play he was writing, i.e. *Twelfth Night, after* rather than *before* the visit.

Internal evidence includes the song that is maltreated by Feste and Sir Toby in Act II Scene 2 (see *Textual Notes*), which is part parody of a popular song current in 1600–01. There are also the passing references to Sir James Shirley's visits to the court of the Shah of Persia between late 1599 and April 1601, though these mentions are oblique, Fabian being prepared to forego a pension from 'the Sophy' in order to watch the 'madness' of Malvolio, and Sir Toby referring to 'Cesario' as a 'fencer to the Sophy'. There were two accounts of the visits published, one of which came out late in 1601. It seems likely that Shakespeare saw either or both, and inserted these topical references into the play as he wrote it.

Other contemporary associations do not help to fix when the play was written, but they do establish that it belonged after 1598. The phrase 'like an icicle on a Dutchman's beard' (Act III Scene 2) refers to the Arctic voyage of the Frieslander William Barentz, an account of which was published in 1598. This probably, because of the conditions it described, provided a talking point for some time. Maria also has a contemporary reference put into her mouth when she speaks of Malvolio smiling 'his face into more lines than is in the new map with the augmentation of the Indies' (Act III Scene 2). This map was in fact issued in 1599 and reissued in 1600, thus establishing that a date earlier than 1599 for the writing of *Twelfth Night* is virtually impossible. There is every reason to believe that the play was in fact written in 1601.

# Scene summaries, commentaries, textual notes and revision questions

## Act I Scene 1

This short scene introduces us to one of the main characters in the ensuing action: Orsino, Duke of Illyria. Surrounded by his attendants, he is pondering on the nature of love. After a punning exchange with Curio, he reveals his love, real or affected, for the lady Olivia, and with the entry of Valentine, whom he has sent to Olivia with a message of love, he learns that that love has been spurned. Olivia is rather excessively mourning the death of her brother but the Duke accepts this as an indication of her quality and capacity to love.

### *Commentary*

There is a certain affected melancholy in Orsino's attitudes; but the ideas of romantic love, sexual appetite and music – all facets of the play – are present here. There is fine natural description ('That breathes upon a bank of violets'), so that though we may be in Illyria we are in fact in the English countryside. The invocation to love sounds one of the keynotes of the play, while the image of the sea looks ironically forward to the following scene; the sea, in a sense, gives Viola to Orsino. The immediacy of the word-play and the employment of the hunting image are also typical of the quick and witty language used. Olivia's excessive mourning and Orsino's excessive invocations to, and expressions of, love underline the romantic elements of the play, both being based on self-indulgence rather than real feelings.

**surfeiting** Being over-filled.
**appetite** i.e. for music as well as love.
**dying fall** (The music) coming to an end, hence dying away.
**sound** i.e. of the music and the wind, the latter in the beautiful natural simile used by Orsino.
**quick** Sharp, lively.
**validity and pitch** Value, whatever value.
**falls into abatement** Is reduced.
**shapes** Images.
**fancy** Imagination, or the lover's imagination.

**high fantastical**  Particularly imaginative; the imagination carried to new heights.

**Why so I do . . .**  Orsino puns on 'hart' (deer) and 'heart' (his own love for Olivia).

**turn'd into a hart**  A reference to the Greek huntsman Actaeon's seeing the goddess Diana bathing, for which offence he was transformed into a stag and torn to death by his own hounds.

**fell**  Savage.

**element**  Air.

**seven years' heat**  The passing of seven summers.

**at ample view**  Openly, fully.

**cloistress**  Nun.

**water once a day**  i.e. weep tears of grief regularly. This is ironic, and suggests that Olivia is exaggerating, making a ritual of her mourning.

**eye-offending brine**  Salt tears that make the eyes sting.

**A brother's dead love**  The love of a brother who is dead. This is explained in the next scene.

**frame**  i.e. calibre.

**golden shaft**  The golden arrow of the God of Love, Cupid.

**kill'd the flock**  An extension of the hunting/killing imagery which marks this scene, strictly meaning here that when she falls in love all other feelings will be overcome.

**liver, brain, and heart**  The seats respectively of love and passion, the intellect and the imagination and of emotion and affection.

**sovereign**  Separate.

**supplied, and fill'd . . . one self king**  (All her attributes) are subservient to love.

**flowers . . . bowers**  Note the rhyming couplet, a favourite Shakespearean device to end, round off a scene.


## Act I Scene 2

Viola, the Captain and some sailors have been shipwrecked on the coast of Illyria. Initially we understand that her brother may have been drowned (note that Olivia too has lost a brother) but the Captain believes that he may have been saved. Viola questions the Captain about the country in which they find themselves, and learns from him of Orsino's love for Olivia and of the latter's vow of chastity after her brother's death. Viola says that she wishes that she could serve Olivia, but learning that Olivia will admit nobody to see her, says that she will disguise herself as 'an eunuch' and serve the Duke Orsino. The Captain agrees to help her in her disguise.

## Commentary

This scene introduces us to Viola, and we are made immediately aware of her love for her brother, of her hope that he will be found alive, and of her enquiring mind. Viola's personality comes over strongly when she muses on the fact that Orsino 'was a bachelor then', almost as if she hopes he is still unmarried, so that she can attach herself to him. She decides that she would like to serve Olivia – sympathy for the latter's situation is immediately shown, for she connects it with her own loss of a brother. Viola's quick switch to the idea of disguising herself leads to one of the major aspects of the play, that of mistaken identity. Viola shows imagination, courage, vivacity and some wit. Note the classical references to Elysium and Arion (see below) and again the light rhyming couplets that end the scene.

**Illyria** Strictly Yugoslavia, but there are many English references which suggest that the name is merely a convenient one for romantic comedy.
**Elysium** Paradise, according to the Greek poets. Viola's quick wit is shown in this half-pun with Illyria.
**Perchance** Perhaps, or merely by (good) chance and note the running word-play here, typical of the play's wit.
**driving** Storm-driven.
**liv'd** Stayed afloat.
**like Arion on the dolphin's back** Arion, Greek minstrel and poet, was captured while returning to Corinth with rich treasure. He was allowed to sing one song before he was cast into the waves; this so fascinated a dolphin that it carried him to safety on its back.
**hold acquaintance with** i.e. keep in touch with, not be overcome by.
**authority** Confirmation.
**The like of him** The same for him, i.e. that like me he may have escaped.
**He was a bachelor then** An indication of Viola's spirit and vivacity, the implication being that if he is still a bachelor he may be interested in her.
**very late** Until recently.
**fresh in murmur** Recent gossip.
**abjur'd** Renounced.
**deliver'd** Revealed.
**Till I had made . . . my estate is** Until I had found that the time was ripe for me to reveal my situation.
**hard to compass** Difficult to accomplish.
**suit** Approach.
**nature . . . pollution** i.e. what appears beautiful often conceals the corruption within.
**suits With** Matches.
**outward character** i.e. what you appear to be.

**bounteously** Generously.
**haply . . . the form of my intent** i.e. may best suit my purpose.
**eunuch** Male servant, here associated with singing.
**many sorts of music** Viola concentrates on this, and in fact music and
  reactions to it are very important in the play.
**allow me very worth** Prove that I am worthy (to serve him).
**shape . . . wit** i.e. make your silence accord with my idea.
**mute** Dumb servant.
**When my tongue . . .** If I talk let me be blinded.

## Act I Scene 3

Sir Toby Belch and Maria in conversation; he is deploring Olivia's
seclusion over her brother's death, while Maria is castigating him
for keeping late hours. Sir Toby spends much of his time drinking, and boasts of his friend, Sir Andrew Aguecheek, 'a foolish
knight' who has been brought to the house as a potential suitor for
Olivia. Maria continues to be critical, saying that Sir Andrew
spends most of his time drunk in Sir Toby's company. When Sir
Andrew enters he certainly appears foolish, and is no match for
Maria, who spiritedly bandies words with him. When Sir Andrew
threatens to go home the next day, Sir Toby tells him that Olivia
will have nothing to do with the Count (Orsino) who is also
wooing her, and Sir Andrew agrees to stay. Sir Toby continues to
mock him, particularly about his dancing.

## *Commentary*

This scene contrasts effectively with the self-induced melancholy
of Orsino and the pathos and vulnerability of Viola's situation.
The comic characters of the sub-plot speak in prose, as befits their
lesser role in the romantic comedy. The scene is rich in punning
and word-play, the exchanges are earthy, witty, and coarse; the
scene may be Illyria, but the references are, many of them (see
below) specifically contemporary and English. The main charac-
teristics are spelled out in the case of Maria – shrewd, witty,
spirited – and of Sir Toby – drunken, loud, opportunist. He eggs
on Sir Andrew and is obviously using him, making fun of his
simplicity and urging him to make himself even more ridiculous

**niece** A close relative.
**care's an enemy to life** i.e. melancholy stops you enjoying life.

**except, before excepted**  A legal phrase meaning 'unless already made an exception'.

**I'll confine**  Sir Toby deliberately takes the word to mean 'put on finery, dress up'.

**ducats**  Elizabethan gold coins.

**he'll have but a year in all these ducats**  i.e. he'll get through all this money within a year.

**viol-de-gamboys**  The violoncello, held between the player's legs.

**without book**  i.e. without understanding or knowledge, a judgement certainly demonstrated after Sir Andrew has uttered a few phrases.

**natural**  Maria is punning, 'natural' being 'idiot'.

**gift**  Note how Maria is referring back to the 'good gifts of nature'.

**gust**  Enjoyment, relish.

**gift of a grave**  Maria continuing the play on 'gift', here indicating that Sir Andrew would be killed in a duel, a subtle look forward to the later 'duel' scene.

**substractors**  Detractors.

**add**  Maria can't resist the pun – a connection with 'substract' or 'subtract', as we would say now.

**coistrel**  Worthless fellow.

**turn o' th' toe**  Spin or pirouette.

**parish top**  A whipping-top kept for the use of villagers, but whether for exercise, entertainment or punishment is uncertain.

*Castiliano vulgo*  A Spanish sounding phrase, which appears meaningless, though such phrases were fashionable after the defeat of the Spanish Armada.

**Agueface**  Perhaps a slip of the tongue, or even an insult.

**shrew**  Punning on the meanings of 'small mammal' and 'bad-tempered, nagging woman'.

**Accost**  Approach, make up to – Sir Toby elaborates in the next few lines the sexual innuendo.

**What's that?**  i.e. the meaning of 'accost'. Sir Andrew is very slow on the uptake.

**undertake her**  Take her on (definite sexual suggestion).

**in this company**  i.e. the audience.

**And . . . so**  If you let her go like that.

**fools in hand?**  Idiots to contend with?

**thought is free**  Think what you wish, you are free to do so.

**buttery bar**  Serving hatch or ledge.

**dry**  A pun on being thirsty *and* impotent.

**barren**  No longer fruitful, emptied.

**canary**  Wine (from the Canary Islands).

**put down**  Another pun, meaning overcome with drink and outsmarted in talk.

**Christian . . . man**  Ordinary man (Sir Andrew often uses too many words).

**And**  If. 'An' is also used to convey 'if'.

22 Twelfth Night

**Pourquoi** French for 'why'. Sir Andrew clearly does not understand. and Sir Toby is mocking Sir Andrew's supposed ability as a linguist, which he himself has praised.

**tongues** Languages, with a pun on 'tongs' for curling hair.

**bear-baiting** A contemporary reference to a common Elizabethan sport.

**Past question** Without doubt.

**flax . . . distaff** Linen fibre on the stick ready for spinning.

**a housewife** A prostitute, with sexual innuendo in keeping with Sir Toby's capacity for bawdy associations.

**none of me** Nothing to do with me, won't entertain my suit.

**there's life in't** There's a chance for you (in paying court to Olivia).

**masques and revels** Theatricals and dances (the performers wore masks) and entertainments, another contemporary reference.

**kickshawses** Generally, unimportant things (from the French *quelques choses*; 'somethings').

**under . . . betters** Apart from those who are more expert than I am.

**galliard** Brisk dance.

**cut a caper . . . the mutton to't** Leap about . . add sauce to it. Sir Toby is punning on 'caper'.

**back-trick** Dance step, but perhaps having sexual associations too.

**Mistress Mall's picture?** Probably a contemporary reference to a painting protected from dust by a curtain.

**coranto** A running dance.

**sink-a-pace** Five-step dance (cinq pas), but Sir Toby's bawdy pun is on 'sink', the open sewer.

**constitution** Shape.

**the star** i.e. astrologically favourable to dancing (the galliard).

**stock** Stocking.

**Taurus** The Bull which. strictly, controls the neck and the throat according to the lore of the Zodiacal signs.

## Act I Scene 4

Viola as Cesario has already been taken into the favour of Orsino who, upon his entrance, sends Viola to undertake the courtship of Olivia on his behalf. Viola, henceforth referred to in the play as Cesario until she is revealed demurs, obviously loath to proceed since she has fallen in love with Orsino.

### Commentary

The theme of love at first sight, central to the romance of *Twelfth Night*, is exemplified here as Viola confesses to herself her love for Orsino. This complements Orsino's expression of his love at first sight for Olivia in Scene 1. This scene has fine poetic qualities, running dramatic irony (since the audience knows that 'Cesario' is a woman and would appreciate Orsino's description of him where 'all is semblative a woman's part') and reveals Viola's vulnerability. Notice that before Orsino enters, the exchange between Valentine and Viola is in prose (they are not yet in noble company); that Viola's advance is so quick that it makes for drama and romance, and that the sending of Viola to Olivia by Orsino shows a certain cunning on his part – he thinks 'he' will succeed because of 'his' attractions and youth. 'He' does succeed but not in the way Orsino hopes for; Olivia falls in love with 'Cesario', thus continuing the love-at-first-sight theme. Orsino again indulges his melancholy by wishing to be alone; note another reference to astrological influence, by which the Elizabethans set much store.

**advanced** Promoted.
**humour** Changes of mood.
**no less but all** Everything.
**unclasp'd . . . the book** Revealed to you my deep feelings.
**address thy gait unto** Take your direction towards.
**fixed foot** Immovable presence.
**civil bounds** Polite behaviour.
**make unprofited return** Coming back without having achieved anything.
**Surprise her** Overcome her.
**dear faith** Sincere love.
**attend** Listen.
**nuncio's** Messenger's.
**belie thy happy years** Falsify your youth.
**That say thou art a man** A superb example of dramatic irony, with Orsino unconsciously hitting the truth.
**Diana's lip** The lip of the moon goddess. Diana in classical mythology was associated with romantic love and beauty.
**rubious** Red, like a ruby.
**small pipe . . . sound . . . part** i.e. Cesario's' voice had not yet broken and was similar to a woman's[!]
**thy constellation is right apt** Astrological signs are in your favour.
**as freely . . . thine** To use (your master's fortunes) as if they were your own.
**barful** Hindering, full of obstacles.
**myself would be his wife** A recognition that she has fallen in love with Orsino (and note the rhyming couplet concluding the scene).

## Act I Scene 5

Maria and the Clown — Feste — are engaged in word-play over his recent absence, before Olivia enters with her steward Malvolio. She has her own exchange with Feste, who generally gets the better of her, and appeals to Malvolio, who pronounces sourly and pompously on Feste. Maria announces that a young gentleman wishes to see Olivia, and the latter sends Malvolio to deal with this, saying that if the gentleman is from Orsino she will not see him. Sir Toby enters 'half drunk', engages in a verbal duel with the Clown; they leave before Malvolio arrives to say that the young gentleman will not take no for an answer. Malvolio's description of him excites Olivia's curiosity and she says that she will receive the young man in the presence of her gentlewoman Maria.

Olivia, veiled, receives Viola, who has prepared what she will say; after a further exchange, Olivia agrees to hear Viola without Maria being there. She unveils, and Viola expresses Orsino's love for her; Olivia rejects it. Viola then says what she would do if she felt for Olivia as Orsino does. Olivia is still intent on refusing Orsino, but is moved by Viola's eloquence. She tells Viola to return to Orsino and says that 'he' ('Cesario') may perhaps come to her again. Viola refuses Olivia's money and departs; Olivia, left alone, reveals that she has fallen in love with 'Cesario'. Intent on seeing 'him' again, Olivia sends Malvolio after Viola with a ring which she says 'Cesario' has left behind. Though she tells Malvolio to make it clear that the Duke has no hope, she cunningly says that if 'Cesario' were to return the next day she would explain to him her reasons for rejecting the Duke

## *Commentary*

This long scene is rich in word play; Olivia, Maria and Feste indulge in punning, Feste additionally in witty reasoning that generally triumphs. Some of his phrases are almost proverbial in their wit and wisdom. As long as Feste and the subordinates remain on stage, the scene is in prose; Viola as subordinate also speaks in prose, but is elevated into verse when she is alone with Olivia, perhaps to mark the 'noble' equality of the two characters. For someone mourning the death of a brother Olivia is singularly spirited, particularly in her verbal duel with Feste; she is also direct and uncompromising with Malvolio when he presumes to put down Feste. The scene contains more than merely verbal comedy, for Sir Toby lives up to his name, and his drunkenness provides buffoonery before the advent of Viola and the raising of the romantic temperature. We note Olivia's curiosity once the appearance of the young gentleman has been described; like Viola she is feminine, romantic, and vulnerable.

Viola almost mars the Duke's suit, perhaps intentionally, by indicating that she has prepared her statement on his behalf, thus undermining its immediacy and reality. She affects not to know which is the 'honourable lady of the house', and Olivia responds by asking if Viola is an actor. She is obviously taken with Viola; she dismisses her servants so that she may be alone with her. She is witty but impressionable, and Viola exceeds her commission with poetic utterance calculated to make inroads into Olivia's feelings. The latter, moved, acknowledges her love for Viola, and uses the trick of the ring in order to get her to come again.

The scene is rich in dramatic irony because of mistaken identity. And there is a superb contrast between Malvolio on the one hand and Feste, Maria and Sir Toby on the other, thus indicating the divisions in Olivia's household which are to provide so much of the action to come. Although Malvolio is pompous, self-opiniated and somewhat vindictive, it is obvious that Olivia greatly respects him; however, she doesn't hesitate to correct him. We feel the pathos of Feste, who has to live by his wits, and Maria's tongue is as sharp as ever. Notice that both heroines are capable of quickly falling in love, Olivia with Cesario/Viola, and Viola with the Duke. The resolution of these loves will occupy the action of the play, and raise dramatic expectation.

**fear no colours**  Be afraid of no enemy.
**Make that good**  Prove that.
**good lenten answer**  Poor reply (meagre, like meals in Lent).
**In the wars . . .**  i.e. you'll need to be brave to say that, since you are in trouble with Olivia through your truancy.
**their talents**  Their abilities. Also a reference to Matthew 25, the parable of the talents, 14–30, which has interesting references linking with the treatment of Malvolio later.
**Many a good hanging prevents a bad marriage**  One of the Clown's proverbial witticisms. with the idea of 'better to be hanged than married' behind it.
**let summer bear it out**  Time will tell. I may go on getting away with it.
**points**  A pun on 'issues' *and* 'laces' for holding up breeches.

**gaskins** Breeches.
**Eve's flesh** i.e. tempting.
**you were best** It would be best for you.
**Wit . . . fooling** The clown Feste prays for inspiration.
**Quinapalus** Name of a supposed philosopher made up by Feste
**dry** Barren and thirsty, as in Act I Scene 3.
**dishonest** Shirking your duties by absenting yourself.
**madonna** My lady
**mend** Improve (cf. mend your ways).
**botcher** Repairer of clothes.
**patched** A reference to his own clothes – the clown's motley.
**syllogism** Argument, like the one he has just used.
**no true cuckold but calamity . . . flower** i.e. grief (calamity) and flower
   (beauty) do not last, a reference to Olivia's mourning for her brother.
**Misprision** i.e. failure to appreciate the point.
*cucullus non facit monachum* 'A cowl does not make a monk', with
   Feste indicating what he wears on his head and what is inside it.
**Dexteriously** Dextrously, skilfully.
**catechise** Cross-question.
**mouse of virtue** A term of endearment, hence some impertinence on
   Feste's part, since he is speaking to Olivia.
**Infirmity, that decays the wise . . .** Age or sickness affects the wise, and
   makes fools even more foolish.
**no fox . . . you are no fool** I'm not cunning or devious, but you're not
   as clever as I am.
**put down . . . ordinary fool** Set beside . . . a tavern fool (with the
   implication that Feste was outdone in wit).
**out of his guard** A fencing term, the metaphor here meaning that
   Feste has no answers.
**minister occasion** Give him the opportunity.
**wise men** i.e. having their faculties.
**set** Predictable.
**zanies** Imitators.
**distempered** Disordered. Olivia goes on to list Malvolio's limitations.
**free disposition** Generous inclinations.
**bird-bolts** Short, blunt-headed arrows. The implication is that
   Malvolio is making a mountain out of a molehill.
**allowed** Professional, free to joke as he wishes.
**rail** Rant abusively.
**discreet** Discerning.
**Mercury** The messenger of the gods; the Deceiver.
**endue thee with leasing** Grant you the ability to lie.
**well attended** Having many servants in attendance on him.
**Fetch him off** Call him away.
**madman** Mad talk, nonsense
**old** Flat. Olivia waits until Malvolio has left before reproving Feste.
**Jove** King of the Gods.

**pia mater**  Brain (literally, the membrane surrounding it).

**sot**  Fool.

**lethargy**  Drowsiness (Olivia is being diplomatic).

**Lechery**  Sir Toby mishears in his drunkenness

**defy**  Deny.

**and he will**  If he wants to.

**all one**  All the same (to me).

**above heat**  Enough to bring on a flush.

**crowner**  Coroner.

**sit**  Consider the case.

**the fool shall look to the madman**  A brilliant and unobtrusive anticipation of Feste's own function later in dealing with the 'mad' Malvolio.

**a sheriff's post**  A post was often fixed outside the house of a sheriff or magistrate as a sign of authority and for the display of notices.

**Why, of mankind**  Note that Malvolio's answers are exasperating Olivia, who with feminine curiosity wants to know more of the 'young gentleman'.

**Not yet . . . boy**  Ironically, Malvolio does say that 'Cesario' is neither man nor boy.

**embassy**  i.e. address.

**which is she?**  Note Viola's affectation of not knowing, which adds to the comedy of the scene and subtly underlines mistaken identity.

**loath to cast away my speech**  i.e. waste what has been so carefully prepared – another ironic shaft at the 'falseness' of courtly love.

**comptible, even to the least sinister usage**  Sensitive, even to the slightest discourtesy.

**out of my part**  i.e. beyond what I have been told to say (but note the reference to 'part' – the actor's role – which is wittily picked up by Olivia).

**my profound heart**  Our colloquial 'Honestly I'm not!' seems nearest to this.

**I am not that I play**  Dramatic irony (this scene is full of it) and wittily referring back to the 'actor' insult.

**If I do not usurp myself**  Unless I am playing a part that is not mine (a continuation of the 'acting' innuendo).

**rather to wonder at**  i.e. to see you for myself, contemplate you.

**'tis not that time of moon with me**  I am not in the mood for madness. (The moon has always been thought to influence 'lunatics' – from the latin word *luna* meaning 'moon').

**skipping**  Flippant.

**hoist sail . . . swabber . . . hull**  Get ready to leave . . . deck-cleaner . . . float. Note Viola's ready wit in continuing this nautical sequence.

**Some mollification for your giant**  Get your guard to calm down; there may be a sarcastic reference to the fact that Maria is very small!

**Tell me your mind**  Do you wish to hear what I have to say. (since I have a message to deliver)?

**the courtesy of it is so fearful**  The awful ceremony (of Viola's prepared speech). Olivia is being sarcastic.

**Speak your office**  Say what it is your duty to say.

**overture**  Declaration.

**taxation of homage**  No financial demand.

**olive**  Symbol of peace.

**as matter**  i.e. as my intention is.

**entertainment**  Treatment (perhaps referring to Sir Toby and Malvolio).

**as secret as maidenhead**  Only be revealed to one person.

**divinity**  Sacred to you.

**to . . . profanation**  i.e. degraded if heard by others.

**comfortable**  Cheering.

**by the method**  i.e. in this way (Viola is continuing the text/chapter analogies by using 'first').

**heresy**  Against the church, but here used to balance the 'divinity' Olivia spoke of a few lines earlier.

**out of your text**  Going beyond what you have been told to say.

**draw the curtain and show you the picture**  Olivia is being coyly sarcastic – but note that in the structure of the play this reference reminds us of 'mistress Mall's picture' in Act I Scene 3.

**sweet and cunning**  Note the ironic contrast – 'sweet' because attractive, and 'cunning' because tempting.

**If you . . . no copy**  i.e. if you will lead a single life and not marry and have a child. Viola is playing on the word 'copy' as reproduction, thus continuing the painting analogy.

**divers schedules**  Various lists (and note that Olivia is speaking in prose, an indication that she is sarcastically 'reducing' everything to a fact.)

**particle . . . to my will**  Everything listed, noted and attached like a codicil to my will – but also playing on the word 'will' – according to my wishes.

**indifferent**  Reasonably.

**praise**  Appraise, set a value on.

**could . . . recompens'd**  Would only be receiving its just reward.

**nonpareil**  Unequalled.

**fertile**  Abundant.

**voices . . . divulged**  Widely spoken of with favour.

**free**  generous.

**deadly life**  Living death.

**I would not understand it**  i.e. I would not accept it.

**Make me . . .**  One of the most beautifully poetic speeches in the play: Viola is indeed an 'actor', and a very accomplished one, but her romantic expression of love, in the Duke's name for Olivia, is of course her own expression of love for the Duke.

**willow**  i.e. the symbol of grief for unrequited love

**my soul**  i.e. she whom I love – Olivia.

**cantons** Songs.

**contemned** Despised, rejected.

**babbling gossip of the air** i.e. the echoing and re-echoing.

**You might do much** i.e. you might achieve much, the innuendo being 'you might move me'

**Above my fortunes, yet my state is well** Higher than my present social position, but I am happy with it.

**To tell me how he takes it** Olivia is using a stratagem to get Viola to come and see her again.

**fee'd post** Messenger who expects to be paid or tipped.

**recompense** Punning on money *and* love.

**Love make his heart . . .** May the one you love be totally unresponsive. This is fine dramatic irony, indicating what must happen when Olivia falls in love with Viola, as she does here.

**Farewell, fair cruelty** Note the rhyming couplet to round off Viola's attack and make an effective exit.

**thou art** The use of the intimate 'thou' indicates Olivia's feelings for Viola.

**five-fold blazon** Olivia has defined Viola's qualities in the previous line; the metaphor is from armorial markings.

**Unless the master were the man** A superbly condensed ambiguity. Olivia is saying 'If only this (Viola) were the master and not the servant', but she is also saying 'Perhaps this *is* the master (Orsino) disguised as a servant.'

**catch the plague?** Fall in love?

**County's** Count's.

**he left this ring . . .** Olivia cannot let herself down before her household, but tells this lie in order to get Viola to return, and also to cover her own feelings for her.

**flatter with** Give a false impression to.

**If that the youth . . .** Notice that Olivia is really telling Malvolio to make sure that the 'youth' himself will be admitted!

**Mine eye . . . mind** I am allowing appearances to deceive me.

**Fate . . . so** We do not control our destiny but must accept fate's decrees, therefore, let things take their course. Note again two rhyming couplets to end the scene and convey Olivia's acceptance of her love and fate.

## Revision questions on Act I

**1** By brief quotation and fuller comment, show what variety is achieved by Shakespeare in the first three scenes of the play.

**2** Write an account of the interview between Olivia and Viola, bringing out the humour and dramatic irony of the scene.

**3** Write a brief character sketch of (a) Maria and (b) Orsino in the action so far.

**4** Compare and contrast Sir Toby Belch and Sir Andrew Ague-cheek and say what they contribute to the humour of this Act.

**5** Write a brief essay on the use of word-play in the first Act of the play.

**6** Write an essay on the effects of mistaken identity in the first Act.

### Act II Scene 1

A very short scene, its object being to introduce us to Sebastian, Viola's twin brother, who has survived the shipwreck; and Antonio, who has saved Sebastian from the sea and who has a strong interest in his welfare  Sebastian reveals that he thinks Viola has been drowned, and, despite Antonio's expressed wish to be his servant, says that he will make his way alone to Orsino's court. When he has gone, Antonio reveals that he (Antonio) has 'many enemies' there  This fact will prove important in the plot.

### Commentary

The dramatic importance of the scene is that it prepares us for most of the ensuing events. There are curious parallels too; like his sister, Sebastian has been rescued by a sea-captain; like her, he makes for Orsino's court, and Antonio's wish to be his servant parallels Viola's position with Orsino. Antonio has a strong, almost possessive love for Sebastian which will later lead to his arrest. The language is prose, as befits Sebastian's lack of status (cf. Viola) in this new land, Antonio's essential nobility of character being revealed at the end of the scene when he speaks in verse. This scene informs both reader and audience while the main action proceeds at the houses of Orsino and Olivia. And it arouses dramatic expectation, since we sense that Sebastian will at some point reappear.

**my stars . . . fate** One of the several references in the play to astrological influence, here with Sebastian implying that his horoscope is such that it might cause evil to fall upon Antonio

**distemper** Adversely influence.

**sooth** Truly

**my determinate voyage .  . extravagancy** The voyage I am undertaking is just a wandering one

**so excellent a touch of modesty**   i.e. you are so considerate and polite.

**extort from me . . . keep in**   Question me about what I wish to keep secret.

**charges me in manners**   Obliges me to return your politeness.

**express myself**   Tell you about myself. (In fact it is essential that the audience has the information too!)

**Messaline**   Imaginary place name, perhaps deriving from Marseilles.

**in an hour**   Within the hour.

**breach**   Waves.

**boldly publish**   Speak freely of.

**bore**   Had.

**with more**   i.e. salt tears.

**bad entertainment**   Your poor reception at my home.

**your trouble**   Your putting yourself out for me.

**If you will not murder me for my love . . .**   It will kill me (if I am not allowed to be your servant) — strong feelings after so short an acquaintance; almost paralleling Viola's quick love for Orsino.

**kill him whom you have recovered**   Sebastian takes up the image used by Antonio courteously, saying that it would 'kill' him to impose further on Antonio.

**kindness**   Warm affection.

**manners of my mother . . . mine eyes . . . tales**   I still feel such grief that, if I'm not careful, I shall cry like a woman and show my inner feelings.

**gentleness**   Blessing.

**I have many enemies . . .**   See note in summary above.

**sport**   i.e. a challenge, again indicative of the strength of Antonio's feelings.

## Act II Scene 2

Malvolio has followed Viola, seeking to return the ring allegedly left by her. Viola of course denies that she gave Olivia a ring; Malvolio throws it down in front of her. Left to herself, Viola bemoans the possibility that Olivia has fallen in love with her; she goes back over their interview, and convinces herself that Olivia exhibited all the signs of passion. She expresses her own equivocal position, spelling out the eternal triangle with a difference and saying she hopes that time will sort things out, i.e. her love for Orsino and his love for Olivia.

### *Commentary*

The ring plot reveals Olivia's feelings clearly to Viola, whose initial exchange with Malvolio shows up his pomposity and self-importance, though he truthfully repeats what Olivia told him to, thus showing a certain conscientiousness. Viola's account of Olivia's reactions reveals her sensitivity, the quality of her observation, her sympathy, though her account is interestingly at variance with what the audience and reader saw and noted between the two. Viola also ponders on the penalties of disguise, thus underlining the mistaken identity aspect of the play.

With the departure of Malvolio, Viola gives poetic utterance to her false position and, like Olivia, determines to leave things to 'time', equivalent to Olivia's conception of 'fate'. Again, a superbly balanced rhyming couplet rounds off the scene. Viola's soliloquy here neatly counterpoints Olivia's speculation about her in Act I Scene 5.

**a desperate assurance**  A despairing certainty.
**hardy**  Bold.
**this**  i.e. Olivia's final rejection of Orsino.
**Receive it so**  Take the ring and these orders.
**She took the ring . . .**  Notice how quickly Viola covers up Olivia's lie to give herself time to think out an explanation of it.
**in your eye**  For you to see clearly.
**outside**  Appearance.
**her eyes had lost her tongue**  i.e. she stared so intently that she couldn't speak.
**the cunning of her passion/Invites me . . .**  Feeling strongly towards me, she has invented this trick to get me to see her again.
**I am the man**  i.e. whom she loves.
**pregnant enemy**  The devil – always ready to take advantage.
**proper false**  Seemingly true and noble, yet deceitful within.
**waxen hearts . . . forms**  Stamps their seals on women's impressionable hearts (the effect produced by attractive men).
**fadge**  Develop, turn out.
**monster**  Viola is outwardly man, inwardly woman, and therefore a 'monster' in her own eyes. The reference also takes in the monstrosity of deception, which she is practising.

### Act II Scene 3

In the early hours of the next morning Sir Toby and Sir Andrew are noisily celebrating; Feste joins them and provides a romantic song. This sets the other two off again, and all continue loudly, until they are interrupted by Maria, who reprimands them for their 'caterwhauling'. Sir Toby does not heed the warning, and Malvolio appears in full steward's majesty. His reprimand is more severe than Maria's, in its implication that Olivia will have Sir Toby turned out of the house if he continues in this vein. Sir Toby and Feste satirize Malvolio in song, and after Feste has left Sir Toby is joined by Maria in insulting Malvolio, who then leaves. Maria then reveals a plan she has concocted in order to humiliate Malvolio. Her idea is to leave a letter in his way which will contain a description of him supposedly written by Olivia, in which she makes no secret of her love for her steward. Maria intends to make sure that Sir Toby and Sir Andrew watch the effect on Malvolio when he finds the letter.

### Commentary

The opening of this scene is full of knockabout humour; the simplicity of Sir Andrew is contrasted with the loud fluency of Sir Toby and, on his entrance, the wit of Feste. The clown's song is poignant and romantic, and Maria's entrance is dramatic, Sir Toby's response tipsily couldn't-care-less, and Malvolio's dignity is certainly affronted by the noise and the insults. At the same time one is compelled to remember that he is doing a job, and though we see him as something of a kill-joy we can never be entirely out of sympathy with him; after all, Olivia's house would be chaotic without him if Sir Toby had his way.

The baiting of Malvolio through the single matching lines of the song of Sir Toby and Feste is effective humour but again there is a sadistic element, remarked on by Malvolio when he observes, 'This is much credit to you'. His intention to tell Olivia seems justifiable in the light of their behaviour, but Maria, who has hitherto tried to exert a restraining influence, reveals an ingenious plan which does credit to her intelligence, if nothing else, after Malvolio has left and she has flung an insult after him. Note that Maria intends to play on Malvolio's vanity, and that the major theme of deception is now being extended, as it will be further when later Malvolio is imprisoned and the clown becomes Sir Topas. As befits the scene and the speakers, the language is in prose; wit, humour, and vivid imagery run throughout the scene, and Maria is revealed as a positive, clever and cunning woman.

**diluculo surgere**  Half of the proverbial phrase 'it is very healthy to get up early'.

**the four elements** Air, water, earth and fire.

**stoup** Flagon.

**'we three'** A picture, sometimes an inn sign, of two asses, hence Feste's opportunist remark.

**a catch** A round or song in which each singer in turn 'catches' on to the words of the previous one.

**breast** i.e. his build gives him a good singing voice.

**had . . . shillings** Would give more than forty shillings to have.

**Pigrogromitus . . . Vapians . . . Queubus** Learned-sounding fictitious names coined by Feste, calculated to impress the simple and ignorant Sir Andrew.

**leman** Sweetheart.

**impeticos thy gratillity** I pocketed your gratuity (with Feste making nonsense of the words himself, knowing that Sir Andrew won't notice the difference.)

**whipstock** Whip-handle – the implication being that Malvolio cannot make himself into a whip to punish Feste.

**Myrmidons** Originally the followers of Achilles, but a term used of any attendants who follow blindly. The phrase seems to be nonsense.

**testril** Sixpenny coin.

**good life** Fun and enjoyment.

**both high and low** A possible reference to Sebastian and Viola.

*sweeting* A term of endearment.

**plenty** Profit.

**stuff** Material (note that the song appeared in a song-book published in 1599).

**mellifluous** Flowing like honey.

**by the nose is dulcet in contagion** This silly metaphor means that if we heard through our nostrils the smell would be sweet.

**welkin** Sky.

**draw three souls out of one weaver** Would have three times the effect on a weaver, many of whom were Calvinist refugees from the Netherlands; they were deeply affected by psalm singing.

**dog at a** Quite a performer.

**By'r Lady** An oath – 'By Our Lady' (the Virgin Mary).

**knave . . . knight** Note the antithetical balance, and Feste's play on the words – Sir Toby is both a knave (in his behaviour) and a knight.

**Cataian** Native of Cathay (China). Obviously intended as a reproach, but it probably shows that Sir Toby is too drunk to be talking anything but nonsense.

**politicians** Schemers.

**a Peg-a-Ramsey** The title of an old song, which may perhaps have contained lines appropriate to describe Malvolio's attitudes.

**consanguineous** Related by blood (drunkenly repeated immediately afterwards).

**Tilly-vally** An expression of contempt, but part of a song.

*There dwelt a man in Babylon . . .* Beginning of a popular ballad.

**Beshrew** Curse.

*the twelfth day of December* Sir Toby, drunk, is probably inaccurate, meaning to sing the carol 'The Twelve Days of Christmas', a small echo of the celebration of 'Twelfth night'.

**wit** Good sense.

**coziers'** Cobblers'.

**mitigation or remorse** Concerned enough for other people to lower (your voices).

**Sneck up!** Go hang yourself!

**round** Blunt.

**nothing allied to your disorders** Not approving of your disorderly behaviour.

**and it would** i.e. if it would.

*Farewell, dear heart* Sir Toby and Feste sing an improvised version of the song – cunningly adapted by Shakespeare – in order to antagonize Malvolio.

**Out o' time, sir?** Addressed aggressively to Malvolio, and queries his accusation (and Maria's) that they have exceeded their time by carousing late.

**cakes and ale** The major ingredients of celebration, and hence disapproved of by Puritans like Malvolio.

**Saint Anne** An oath, perhaps to further annoy the religious Malvolio

**ginger** Spice for ale.

**give means** i.e. provide alcohol.

**uncivil rule** Disorderly conduct.

**Go shake your ears** As a donkey does (Malvolio is an ass).

**challenge him the field** i.e. to a duel; reference that unobtrusively anticipates the duel scene

**gull him into a nayword** Deceive him so that he will look a complete fool.

**common recreation** General laughing-stock.

**exquisite** Sir Toby chooses a difficult word – for him to pronounce and for Sir Andrew to understand – in order to mock Sir Andrew's pronouncement.

**constantly** Consistently.

**time-pleaser** We would say 'time-server'.

**affectioned** Affected.

**cons state without book . . . great swarths** Learns high-sounding phrases by heart and uses them greatly whenever he can ('swarths': swathes).

**obscure epistles** Ambiguous letters.

**on a forgotten matter . . .** When neither of us can recall who wrote what, we can't readily recognize the writing – whether it was hers or mine.

**a horse of that colour** Just like that.

**your horse now . . .** Sir Andrew catches on intelligently here!

**Ass, I doubt not**  Maria is not only agreeing with Sir Andrew but referring to the fact that he is an 'ass' too.

**physic**  Medicine.

**construction**  Interpretation.

**Penthesilea**  Queen of the Amazons, hence a joke at Maria s small size but a tribute to her fighting qualities.

**Before me**  My goodness.

**beagle**  The smallest English hound (hence another reference to Maria's stature).

**recover . . . a foul way out**  i.e. (if I don't) win Olivia, (I am) in trouble (because of the money and time wasted).

**cut**  Fool, but a pun on a docked horse (one that has its tail cut) and a coarse reference to the female genitals, a reference developed in Act II Scene 5.

**burn some sack**  Warm up some Spanish wine.

## Act II Scene 4

The Duke, still melancholy, calls for music from Viola, but Curio points out that such singing requires the presence of Feste; while they wait for him, Orsino tells Viola of his own constancy in love, the music in the background contributing to the mood. Viola admits that she loves too, and Orsino is moved to continue his remarks upon the nature of love, saying that the man should be older than the woman and underlining the fact that women's beauty fades. Feste enters, sings a melancholy song in keeping with the Duke's mood and, after being paid, leaves Orsino and Viola alone. Orsino urges Viola to visit Olivia again and reiterate his love for her, asserting that no woman's love can be as strong as his feeling for Olivia. Viola reveals her own constancy in love obliquely but, questioned by the Duke about her 'sisters' love, pleads ignorance, and is ordered by Orsino to take a jewel to Olivia.

### *Commentary*

Music is at the heart of *Twelfth Night*, and the Duke's romanti: wish for it, together with the nature of Feste's song, underpins the affectation of melancholy that is one of the play's themes. Orsino is in love with love; Viola, in love with Orsino, gives pathetic emphasis to the dramatic irony that runs throughout the scene, since Viola's 'My father had a daughter lov'd a man' is, unbeknown to Orsino, herself. There is further irony in the fact that Orsino asserts constancy, but is later to abandon it, and there are indications here of his fondness for the 'boy' who is to be retransformed into a woman. Orsino, in urging that a woman should take a man older than herself, is unknowingly forecasting his own union with Viola, and their discussion of love is encompassed by irony. Orsino acknowledges that men's 'fancies' change, while Feste's song is a poignant parody of melancholy love, thus an oblique snipe at Orsino, who is enjoying just such a state. Feste continues his innuendo after being paid by Orsino. Viola daringly almost reveals herself ('Say that some lady, as perhaps there is . . .') and provokes Orsino into a male-superiority harangue about man's capacity to love being much greater than woman's. Orsino's self-indulgence and conceit are revealed, and this balances the pathos of Viola's situation. Note the beautiful blank verse poetry of Viola's 'confession' of her love; the word-play, which again runs through the scene; and the rounding-off couplet that concludes it.

**but** Just.
**old and antic** Antiquated, out-dated.
**passion** i.e. sufferings in love.
**light airs and recollected terms** Trivial tunes with their trite phrases.
**giddy-paced** Fast-moving.
**Unstaid** Unstable.
**motions** Feelings.
**It gives . . . thron'd** It captures exactly what is deeply felt in the heart.
**masterly** Expressively.
**favour** Face.
**by your favour** If you like, but Viola is deliberately punning on the Duke's 'face', which she does indeed like.
**your complexion** i.e. like you to look at and with your temperament.
**wears** The metaphor is from clothes, and means 'suits, comes to fit'.
**sways she level** i.e. becomes the stabilising element.
**giddy and unfirm** Unstable and inconstant.
**worn** i.e. worn out, another clothes reference.
**think it well** Believe it.
**hold the bent** i.e. stand the pressure – the metaphor being from archery, the degree of strain that the bow can take.
**display'd** Fully open.
**To die** Viola, continuing the metaphor, means 'To fade', but doubtless she has her own position in mind – she is 'dead' to Orsino because he doesn't know that she's a woman, and also because he loves someone else.

**spinsters** Spinners (the original meaning of the word, which to us now means an unmarried woman).

**free** Unattached.

**silly sooth** Plain truth (this is a comment on Orsino's own judgement, for in reality it is plain self-indulgence).

**dallies with** Lingers upon.

**the old age** i.e. former times when everything was ideal.

*Come away* i.e. come to me quickly.

*sad cypress* A coffin made from the wood of the cypress.

*Fie* Go.

*My part of death* My fate to die.

**pleasure will be paid** We have to pay for our pleasures later.

**leave to leave thee** Orsino, impatient with Feste, takes an over-polite dismissive tone. Feste is soon revenged.

**the melancholy god** Saturn.

**changeable taffeta** Silk so woven that it seems to change colours when seen from different angles.

**opal** A jewel that apparently changes colour in different lights.

**I would have . . . nothing** This sarcastic speech by Feste means that men's moods are like the moods of the sea, which carries everything everywhere, and such men being put to sea would have their business to attend to instead of making a great deal of noise about nothing.

**give place** i.e. leave.

**sovereign cruelty** An unwitting echo (since Orsino doesn't know what was said) of Viola's last words to Olivia in Act I Scene 5 ('fair cruelty').

**the world** Society in general.

**parts** i.e. her position and money.

**as giddily as fortune** As lightly as chance or fate.

**miracle and queen of gems** Her overwhelming attraction.

**pranks** Displays.

**sides** Rib-cage.

**bide** Withstand.

**retention** i.e. the ability to keep down so much love.

**motion** Feeling.

**surfeit, cloyment, and revolt** Having too much, being too full, and then being sick.

**owe** Feel.

**let concealment . . .** Viola is of course describing her own plight.

**a worn i' th' bud** The canker worm in the rose.

**damask** Pink (like the rose).

**green and yellow** She became pale, faded.

**Patience on a monument** Like a statue or allegorical figure which appears to smile bravely at suffering.

**Our shows are more than will** i.e. we display, make a show of more love than we really prove by our actions.

**And all the brothers too** Pathos, for Viola is still subconsciously thinking of her 'dead' brother.

**and yet I know not**  She is not sure that Sebastian is dead.
**give no place**  Not be dismissed
**bide no denay**  Take no denial

## Act II Scene 5

This provides a striking contrast to the previous scene; we are back in the sub-plot to gull Malvolio, and Fabian, who has been reported by Malvolio for bear-baiting, joins Sir Toby and Sir Andrew in anticipation of what is to come. Maria orders them to observe Malvolio from a box-tree; Malvolio enters in complacent mood, already thinking aloud on his prospects with Olivia. As he speaks there are interjections from the group in the box-tree, and Malvolio develops his ideas of his future state. They include the reprimanding of Sir Toby for consorting with Sir Andrew and for drinking; he finds the letter, and is easily duped into thinking that it is from Olivia, conveniently recalling 'evidence' from the past to prove that Olivia loves him. He intends to do what 'she' asks, which will of course make him ridiculous

### *Commentary*

This is the funniest scene in the play, and it moves quickly into comic action. Maria confirms her ingenuity, and the interaction of box-tree comments on the vanity of Malvolio, his conceit, pomposity and gullibility, makes for quick-fire humour with an edge of cruelty. Particularly witty is the look into the future, with Sir Toby fuming and Malvolio in the highest degree of complacency. The whole scene is in prose, the language vivid, alternately plain and direct or with an appropriate metaphor ('here comes the trout that must be caught with tickling'). The verses and the letter are full of clues which point Malvolio in the direction he already wishes to take.

**scruple**  Scrap.
**sheep-biter**  i.e. Malvolio, who attacks the pleasures of others just as dogs bite sheep.
**bear-baiting**  A popular Elizabethan sport, much condemned by the Puritans, hence Malvolio's action.
**it is pity of our lives**  i.e. we should be ashamed to live.
**metal of India**  i.e. Maria is worth her weight in gold
**a contemplative idiot**  Mindless fool.

**Close** Get well hidden.

**tickling** The bait of flattery. A trout can be caught by carefully tickling it so as to lull it into a false security.

**she** Olivia.

**affect me** Liked me, looked up to me.

**come thus near** i.e. say so much.

**uses** Treats.

**follows her** Serves her.

**a rare turkey-cock** Completely self-important.

**jets . . . plumage** Struts . . . his puffed out feathers (a continuation of the turkey-cock image).

**'Slight** An oath, a contraction of 'God's light'.

**The Lady of the Strachey . . . wardrobe** The general meaning is 'A lady who married beneath her station'.

**Jezebel** i.e. a painted, forward woman, after the Biblical character of that name. Sir Andrew hasn't the faintest idea what it means.

**blows him** Inflates him.

**state** A chair suitable to his status.

**stone-bow** Catapult.

**branched** Embroidered (with designs of branches and leaves).

**the humour of state** The air of authority.

**travel of regard** Slow look round.

**play with my . . .** He was about to say 'chain', forgetting that he would no longer be a steward when he married Olivia. It is a neat realistic touch.

**cars** Chariots – an emphasis by Fabian on the difficulty of keeping quiet while listening to Malvolio's fantasies.

**quenching my familiar regard . . .** Stopping my easy smile with a cold look of authority.

**scab** A word of insult.

**the sinews of our plot** i.e. the success of our deception.

**the woodcock near the gin** The bird nears the trap (the woodcock was thought to lack intelligence, and was thus easily trapped).

**spirit of humours** The guardian spirit of men's moods

**intimate** Suggest.

**Her C's, her U's and her T's . . . great P's** A punning sequence, all bawdy. See note on *cut* p.36, great P's being copious urination, piss.

**in contempt of question** Without doubt.

**impressure** Impression from a seal.

**Lucrece** The ring had a representation of Lucrece on it; Shakespeare wrote a narrative poem about her. She was raped by Tarquin.

**liver and all** Completely, passionately.

**numbers** The metre, which changes in the next lines read out by Malvolio.

**brock** Badger.

***a Lucrece knife*** Lucrece stabbed herself after the rape.

***M.O.A.I.*** The letters are calculated to set Malvolio thinking of himself as the beloved, since each of these occurs in his name

**sway my life** Rule me, influence me.

**fustian** Pretentious.

**dressed him** Got ready for him.

**the staniel checks at it** The kestrel wheels towards it. Note the contemporary reference to a popular Elizabethan sport, falconry.

**formal capacity** Average intelligence.

**obstruction** Difficulty.

**position** Order.

**O ay** O I, the last letters of Malvolio's name reversed, as indeed he is being reversed here.

**cold scent** Another contemporary reference to hunting, meaning here 'having little to go on'.

**Sowter will cry upon 't for all this . . .** The dog (called Sowter) will howl excitedly at his discovery, though the real clue is as powerful as the smell of a fox.

**faults** A break in the scent.

**consonancy in the sequel** Agreement with what follows.

**that suffers under probation** It doesn't stand up to examination.

**detraction at your heels** i.e. suffering coming after you.

**simulation** Riddle.

**crush . . . bow** Concentrate . . . reveal.

*inure thyself* Make yourself ready.

*cast thy humble slough* Remove, get rid of your humbleness (as a snake gets rid of its skin).

*opposite* Awkward, perverse.

*tang arguments of state* Loudly speak of important topics.

*the trick of singularity* Affect differences of behaviour and attire.

*yellow stockings . . . cross-gartered* Perhaps fashionable, but Malvolio as a conscientious Puritan in a house of mourning would certainly not have worn them. Olivia dislikes them anyway, as we know from Maria.

**champaign** Countryside.

**discovers** i.e. reveals.

**baffle** Outwit.

**gross acquaintance** Low company.

**point-device** Perfectly.

**jade** Throw over.

**excites to this** Conforms.

**injunction** Order.

**habits** Clothes.

**strange, stout** Reserved, proud.

**even with the swiftness of putting on** i.e. as soon as I can get them on.

**Sophy** The Shah of Persia. This is a contemporary reference to an English explorer who received extravagant gifts from the Shah for diplomatic service (see 'Date').

**thy foot o' my neck?** As a sign of subjection, like a slave.

**tray-trip** A game of dice. 'Tray' means 'three', hence Sir Toby is prepared to gamble with his freedom.

**he must run mad**  A poignant anticipation of what Malvolio is made to appear to be later.
**work upon him**  Fool him, take him in completely.
**aqua-vitae**  Alcoholic spirits.
**notable contempt**  Greatly despised figure.
**Tartar**  Tartarus, the infernal regions of Greek mythology.
**one**  i.e. one of the party.

## Revision questions on Act II

**1**  Write an essay on the use of pathos *and* dramatic irony in this act.
**2**  With particular reference to Scenes 3 and 4, comment on the role of the Clown (Feste) in this act.
**3**  In what ways is Act II, Scene 1 important? You may refer to other parts of the play in your answer.
**4**  Write an essay on the nature of the comedy in Act II Scene 5, bringing out clearly the nature of Maria's plot.
**5**  Write an essay on the characters of Maria *and* Malvolio as they are revealed in this act.

## Act III Scene 1

Again Shakespeare employs contrast, since this scene has none of the excellent if somewhat cruel humour of the previous one. Viola and Feste engage in verbal quibbles, with Viola able to hold her own. She pays Feste and awaits the arrival of Olivia; the latter enters with Maria, but not before Viola has had a short exchange with Sir Toby and Sir Andrew. Olivia insists on being left alone with Viola (who is of course there to continue Orsino's wooing of Olivia). Olivia reveals her deception over the ring and begs Viola to speak on her own account. After a further exchange she also reveals her love for 'Cesario'; Viola, panic-stricken by the revelation, leaves quickly as Olivia continues to confess her love.

### *Commentary*

The ever-present dramatic irony, the brilliant word-play of Feste and Viola, with puns and innuendo as the staple diet, characterize the early part of this scene, Viola displaying humanity in her recognition of Feste's function as a professional fool. Viola's greeting of Olivia is in keeping with her role, for she uses inflated language, which puts the listening Sir Andrew out of countenance — remember that he is a potential suitor for Olivia's hand too, ridiculous though it seems. Viola continues to perform her courtly role, calling Olivia 'fair Princess'. Olivia moves from hints of her love for Viola to outright frankness, and her admission about the ring shows an honesty of nature and a kind of humility; Viola, ever vulnerable and susceptible, is moved to pity her, and this elicits from Olivia a generous reply — that she will not force 'Cesario' to marry her. But she persists in trying to draw out Viola's opinion of her, and Viola's counter is, as ever, in ambiguous word-play which conceals the truth. The dramatic irony has a moving poignancy here, as Olvia in an aside reveals an emotional response to Viola and then, openly and expressively, speaks her love; Viola still has her refuge in her mistaken identity.

**Save thee**  God save thee, a polite greeting.
**tabor**  A small drum, part of the stock-in-trade of professional fools.
**live by . . . stand by . . . lies by**  Typical of the word-play of this scene — and of *Twelfth Night* generally — a succession of puns. 'Lies' and 'stand' both carry sexual innuendo.
**chev'ril**  Kid.
**dally nicely**  Play cleverly.
**words are very rascals, since bonds disgraced them**  No one feels that he has to keep his word unless he has given his bond as well, and this makes the word worthless.
**the orb**  The earth.
**the fool should be as oft with your master . . . mistress**  i.e. I should spend as much time at Orsino's house as at Olivia's, (but with the implication that Orsino and Olivia are equally foolish).
**your wisdom**  A mock courtesy title, almost like 'your worship'.
**pass upon me**  Make me look silly.
**expenses**  Euphemism for a 'tip'.
**commodity**  Consignment.
**sick for one**  i.e. Orsino (a good piece of dramatic irony).
**a pair of these have bred**  i.e. the coins received in the tip. The idea is of (a) getting more money and (b) receiving interest by lending.
**Lord Pandarus of Phrygia . . . Cressida . . . Troilus**  Pandarus was the go-between who arranged the meetings between the ill-starred lovers, Troilus and Cressida, subject of a play by Shakespeare and a long poem by Chaucer. Presumably Feste is offering to bring Olivia to Viola.
**Cressida was a beggar**  This follows all the punning on begged, begging, beggar; Cressida became one, but the irony is that this Cressida – Olivia – will beg Viola for her opinion of her.

**conster** Explain (mock heroic word).

**out of my welkin** Beyond my reach.

**haggard** Wild hawk.

**check at every feather** Seize every chance of a joke (and a tip).

***Dieu vous garde*** God save you.

***Et . . . serviteur*** And you also; (I am) your servant.

**encounter** Go towards (the word is affected court style).

**bound to** Going to; also, beholden to.

**list** Destination.

**Taste** Try.

**understand** Viola puns again; 'understand' means 'are under me, raise me, I stand on them' and they move as she wills, they 'understand' her needs.

**most pregnant and vouchsafed ear** Ready and willing.

**I'll get 'em all three ready** i.e. I'll learn them so that I can use them myself.

**Your servant's servant . . .** Viola's ready wit means 'Orsino is your servant, I am his servant, therefore I am your servant'.

**music from the sphere** As the spheres of the solar system revolved around the earth they were thought to produce beautiful music, but it was only rarely heard by human ear.

**hard construction** Unfavourable opinion.

**sit** Accept passively.

**honour at the stake** The meaning is clear, but this is another reference to the contemporary sport of bear-baiting.

**th' unmuzzled thoughts** This continues the reference. Olivia fears that Viola will think badly of her for so easily revealing her feelings.

**receiving** Insight.

**cypress** Piece of material from Cyprus.

**degree . . . grize** i.e. on the way to love.

**vulgar proof** Commonly shown.

**If one should be a prey . . .** If one has to be seized (by love) then how much better to love the best!

**westward ho!** The audience would recognize this, the cry of Thames watermen as they touted for passengers.

**That you do think . . .** You are forgetting your position (by loving someone beneath you).

**I would have you be** i.e. in love with me.

**for now I am your fool** You are using me, taking up my time.

**Love's night is noon** i.e. love will be revealed anyway – a prelude to Olivia's confession of hers.

**maidhood** Virginity.

**maugre** In spite of (French *malgré*).

**wit** i.e. good sense.

**extort . . . clause** Do not conclude from what I have just said.

**For that** That just because.

**cause**  Reason to woo me.
**reason . . . fetter**  Use this argument.

## Act III Scene 2

This short scene has Sir Andrew doing his best to leave, since he feels that Viola has achieved more success with Olivia than he has, but it is forcefully pointed out by Fabian that Olivia was doing this to stimulate him, Sir Andrew, to his proposal. The sub-plot quickens, as Sir Toby and Fabian persuade Sir Andrew to write a challenge to Viola, Sir Toby intending to press the matter on with Viola. As this second gulling gets under way, Maria enters to report on the first, the ridiculous spectacle of Malvolio in yellow stockings, cross-gartered, and smiling.

### *Commentary*

This short scene is crucial to the sub-plot, the duping of Sir Andrew leading ultimately to an interaction with the main plot and the revelations of identity; the humour is crisp, with Fabian taking a positive role. The idea of the duel promises as much sport as the gulling of Malvolio. Maria's news raises the dramatic anticipation of audience and reader. Sir Toby is shown as an unscrupulous sponge, and he and Fabian as irresponsible jokers living for what they can get out of the present.

**venom**  A term of contempt. 'Venom' – spirit – is the last thing Sir Andrew has.
**orchard**  Garden.
**argument**  Confirmation.
**prove it legitimate**  Demonstrate that you are (a) an ass and (b) that Olivia loves you.
**brimstone in your liver**  Arouse strong feelings.
**fire-new from the mint**  Not yet in circulation, original. Obviously ironic, since Sir Andrew always copies or repeats.
**double gilt**  Twice plated, valuable (an extension of the coin image).
**sailed into the north**  i.e. being coldly treated.
**a Dutchman's beard**  This is a reference to Barentz's expedition to the Arctic in 1696–7.
**policy**  Cunning.
**as lief**  As soon.
**Brownist**  Member of a Puritan sect founded by Robert Brown.
**eleven**  Sir Toby is merely exaggerating the number of wounds.

**commendation** Success.

**curst** Bold.

**the licence of ink** Freedom of words (but note that they are written, not spoken).

**thou'st him** It was insulting to use 'thou' except by agreement, though Sir Toby uses the term frequently to Sir Andrew, perhaps a mark of his real contempt for him.

**lies** Accusations of lying.

**bed of Ware** A famous bed of the period belonging to the inn at Ware in Hertfordshire; it could hold twelve people.

**gall** Bitterness.

**goose-pen** The quill, but also note that Sir Andrew is a 'goose – or a 'natural', as he would put it.

**cubiculo** Small bedroom, cubicle.

**dear** Costly (Sir Toby has succeeded in obtaining much money from Sir Andrew).

**mainropes** i.e. the ropes of the waggon pulled by the oxen.

**hale** Haul.

**so much . . . flea** The amount of blood in the liver was supposed to indicate a person's courage.

**opposite** Opponent.

**presage** Hint.

**spleen** Fit, i.e. if you want to laugh yourself silly.

**renegado** i.e. he has changed his religion.

**passages of grossness** Exaggerated parts of the letter.

**villainously** Hideously.

**like a pedant . . .** Like a schoolmaster (who hadn't got his own school).

**the new map with the augmentation of the Indies** A reference to the 1599 map, which incorporated the East Indies, with grid-lines throughout.

## Act III Scene 3

Another short scene, its object being to update us on Sebastian and Antonio; in a sense it raises dramatic expectation and delays it, since we should naturally wish to see the effect produced by Malvolio. Antonio, fearing for Sebastian's safety, has followed him; Sebastian proposes to explore the town but Antonio, mindful of his own danger, explains how he has offended Orsino by his piracy in the past. He gives Sebastian his purse in case he wants to buy anything, then goes to arrange for their lodgings. The reference to an English inn sign shows that 'Illyria' has the marks of contemporary England.

## Commentary

The scene is undistinguished, Antonio's love and Sebastian's repetition of thanks both lacking depth or even conviction. It is important to the plot, however, for Sebastian is to be mistaken for his sister, and Antonio is to be arrested and have Viola deny him, a telling dramatic incident in the mistaken identity context. It is also important since Antonio's past must be explained if the later part of the plot is to be convincing. The giving of the purse is also important, making Antonio's 'betrayal' by Viola even more moving.

**jealousy** Worry.
**skilless** i.e. having no knowledge of.
**shuffled off with such uncurrent pay** Accepted in return for a valueless payment. The point is that Sebastian has no money, and Antonio is quick to lend him his purse.
**worth** i.e. in terms of money.
**relics** Monuments, famous buildings.
**renown** Make famous.
**the Count his galleys** The Count's galleys.
**ta'en** Captured.
**scarce be answered** Not be possible for me to make amends.
**Belike** Perhaps.
**quality** Nature.
**answer'd** Made up for.
**traffic's sake** In the interests of our trade.
**stood out** Resisted, refused to give in.
**be lapsed** Be captured.
**pay dear** i.e. pay with my life.
**Hold** Wait.
**the Elephant** The inn sign.
**bespeak our diet** Order our food.
**beguile** Pass.
**have me** Find me.
**toy** Small article.
**store** Funds.
**idle markets** Casual shopping.

## Act III Scene 4

Olivia, with Maria, is pondering on her invitation to Viola to visit her. She feels that Malvolio who is 'sad and civil' will suit her mood, when Maria reports that Malvolio is coming, but in a very strange manner. As he enters he appears to think that he and Olivia have some understanding. This of course fits in with the letter, and Malvolio quotes from the letter in support of his behaviour. A servant announces the arrival of Viola, and Maria leaves. Olivia asks that Malvolio should be looked after by Sir Toby and her people, since she values him (Malvolio) highly. This is of course interpreted by Malvolio in the light of the letter which urged him, among other things to 'be opposite with a kinsman'. Sir Toby, Fabian and Maria appear and urge Malvolio to free himself from the devil's influence. Sir Toby is particularly condescending and, when Malvolio has left, the three conspire to have him kept in a dark room because of his 'madness'.

Meanwhile Sir Andrew appears with his written challenge to Viola, a ridiculous letter which reveals his simplicity of mind and his cowardice, and which Sir Toby says he will deliver to Viola. He intends in reality to give a word-of-mouth account to Viola of Sir Andrew's bravery. He and Fabian give way when Olivia comes in with Viola; she gives her a miniature of herself to wear, but Viola requests that she love her master instead. Olivia leaves, telling Viola to come again the next day. Viola, confronted by Sir Toby and Fabian, now receives an account of how Sir Andrew is 'a devil in private brawl'; she replies that she is no fighter, but Sir Toby leaves Fabian with her while he goes in search of Sir Andrew. Fabian cunningly says that he will try to make peace on Viola's account, and Sir Toby enters, playing the same trick on Sir Andrew as he has played on Viola; that is, he builds up Viola's prowess.

Sir Andrew tries to get out of the duel, as does Viola, when Antonio enters, draws his sword, and is on the point of fighting with Sir Toby when he is arrested by Orsino's officers. Thinking that Viola is Sebastian he asks for his purse – Viola is bewildered but offers him money – whereupon Antonio denounces him as 'Sebastian' before he is led away by the officers. Viola now has hope that her brother is alive. When she has left, Sir Toby speaks of her as a coward and urges Sir Andrew on.

## Commentary

This fine scene embodies both main plot and two sub-plots, and sets them into interaction with each other; dramatic irony is present throughout. Malvolio, deluded, obeys the letter and appears ridiculous to the audience and of course to Olivia. Each quotation from the letter adds to the humour and grotesqueness of the exchange, but we should note that Oliivia obviously values Malvolio highly. The humouring of Malvolio is also funny, though there is a sick element to it, almost as if the joke has been carried too far, as indeed later it is. The references to the devil are particularly injurious in view of Malvolio's puritanical beliefs, and the idea of imprisoning him in a dark room smacks of vengeance and gives us the darker side of the comedy of *Twelfth Night*.

The real quality of this scene is shown in its movement, the switching from one level of comedy to another; Sir Andrew's ridiculous challenge is elevated by Sir Toby and Fabian into an ingenious contrivance to make those fight who have no wish to fight; the build-up in the minds of each that their adversary is fearsome is ironically underpinned by the fact that Sir Andrew is a coward and Viola is a woman. It is heightened too by the brief exchange between Olivia and Viola which leaves Viola alone and vulnerable. The effects of delusion are strongly felt in this scene. Note also the *variety* in this scene of language and action and, particularly, the subtle way in which mistaken identity influences the actions and reactions of the characters in both plot and sub-plot.

**him** Viola.

**bestow of** Give to.

**For youth is bought more oft . . .** i.e. I may be able to win him (Viola) to my love by giving him expensive gifts . . . a cynical comment, and hardly applicable to the character of Viola.

**sad and civil** Serious and controlled (fine irony, for now he is not).

**fortunes** Current state of mind (a reference to her mourning).

**tainted in's wits** i.e. has lost his reason

**sad and merry madness** i.e. her madness is sad  Malvolio's merry, yet they are the same.

**sad occasion** Serious matters.

**sonnet** Song.

**'Please one, and please all'** From a contemporary ballad, meaning here 'if it's good enough for one (you), it's good enough for everyone else (including me)'.

**the sweet Roman hand** The style of writing, italic.

**go to bed** i.e. rest (until you are well again. Malvolio takes it as an invitation).

**At your request . . . daws!** Presumably an answer to Maria, not Olivia, Why should I (a nightingale) reply to a jackdaw like you (Maria).

**entreat him back** Persuade him to return.

**miscarry** Have an accident.

**near me** i.e. to understanding.

**consequently** Afterwards.

**habit** Style.

**limed** Caught (as bird in bird-lime).

**'fellow'** Obviously Malvolio takes this as a compliment, raising his status above that of steward.

**dram** One eighth of an ounce, a very small amount.

**incredulous or unsafe** Unforeseen or uncertain.

**full prospect** Fulfilment.

**drawn in little** Within him (Malvolio).

**Legion** See Mark 5, 8–9 for this reference to the 'unclean spirit'.

**man** Fabian's familiarity is intended to exasperate Malvolio, who, as we remember, has reported him for bear-baiting.

**private** Privacy.

**hollow** Referring to the affectation of dignity in his voice.

**and . . . at** If . . . to.

**Carry his water . . .** Take a sample of his urine for analysis to one who can combat witchcraft, a 'wise woman'.

**bawcock** Good fellow (note the tone) from French 'beau coq' – fine rooster'.

**chuck** Chicken.

**biddy** Chicken (Sir Toby is treating Malvolio like a child).

**gravity** The serious-minded.

**play at cherry-pit** A children's game in which cherry-stones were flung into a hole or pit.

**Satan . . . collier** Both references to 'blackness', the first the black arts of the devil, the second the appearance of the coalman.

**If this were played . . .** Another stage reference, this time with the added irony that it is being 'played' and that the 'improbable fiction' is reality before their eyes – and the eyes of the audience.

**genius** Essential soul.

**infection of the device** Fully deceived by the plan.

**take air, and taint** Goes bad, though exposure. Maria is anxious to keep up the pressure.

**the house . . . quieter** i.e. when he has been removed from it.

**in a dark room and bound** The common way of dealing with lunatics.

**carry it thus** Keep up the idea.

**bring the device to the bar** i.e. come into the open with it. Unconscious irony, since courts also give judgement.

**crown thee for a finder of madmen** Make you coroner to pronounce on cases of this kind.

**But see, but see!** Talking of madmen, look who's coming!

**sense-less** Fabian means that Sir Andrew is talking nonsense – indeed the whole challenge is a nonsense.

**Good** Fabian's sarcasm again – a pointed picking up of Sir Andrew's idiocy.

**Thou kill'st . . . villain** Ambiguous, meaning either Sir Andrew or Viola.

**windy side** i.e. safe side.

**my hope is better** i.e. I hope that I'll live – but really he is saying that he hopes he is damned, another typical contradiction.

**scout me** Keep a look-out.

**orchard** See note p.45.

**bum-baily** Bailiff.

**approbation than ever proof itself** Extravagant praise.

**excellently ignorant** Note Sir Toby's exact use of paradox, which contrasts so tellingly with Sir Andrew's misuse.

**clodpole** Blockhead.

**cockatrices** Basilisks which could kill with a look.

**give them way** i.e. keep out of their way.

**unchary** Without caution.

**jewel . . . picture** i.e. a miniature (of Olivia).

**That honour sav'd may upon asking give?** That may be given when asked for with no loss of honour?

**That defence thou hast . . .** Whatever defence you have, see that you use it.

**intercepter** Opponent.

**Dismount thy tuck** i.e. unsheathe your sword.

**yare** Speedy.

**can furnish man withal** Everything that a man can have (of courage and power).

**dubbed . . . carpet consideration** Knighted with an unused rapier for peaceful service (not service in battle).

**incensement** Anger.

**pangs of death and sepulchre** i.e. by killing (you).

**Hob, nob** The same as 'give't or take't', indicating that he's not afraid to die

**conduct** i.e. safe conduct.

**taste** Test.

**competent injury** i.e. an insult that demands repayment.

**meddle** Fight.

**forswear to wear iron** Stop carrying your sword.

**something of my negligence . . .** i.e. something not meant, and certainly not deliberate.

**arbitrement** Clash, conflict.

**to read him by his form** Judging from his outward appearance.

**bound** Obliged.

**firago** Warlike woman, virago.

**pass** Trial bout.

**stuck in** Lunge.

**mortal motion** Deadly thrust.

**answer . . . surely** i.e. returns thrust for thrust.

**Sophy** See note p.41.

**Pox on't** An oath or curse.

**and I thought** If I thought.

**motion** Proposition.

**the perdition of souls** i.e. killing, and going to hell.

**take up** Make up.

**is as horribly conceited** Has a similar fearful impression.

**supportance** Upholding.

**A little thing . . .** Slight sexual innuendo, since Viola is not male.

**duello** Rules of duelling.

**undertaker** i.e. accepts a challenge.

**for that I promised you** i.e. my horse.

**office** Duty.

**favour** Face.

**answer it** i.e. pay for it.

**My having** i.e. . . . what I have.

**my present** i.e. the money I have with me.

**coffer** Strong box for money, here ironic as showing Viola's small amount.

**my deserts to you** i.e. what you owe me (for saving you).

**unsound** Weak and self-pitying.

**Relieved him with such sanctity of love** Saved him by my complete devotion to him.

**image** Noble appearance.

**venerable** i.e. capable of being worshipped. The use of 'idol' and 'god', as well as the preceding 'sanctity' and 'image' ironically underline appearance and reality.

**good feature** Handsome appearance.

**unkind** Cold and unnatural (note the rhyming couplets – Antonio is 'ending' his scene emphatically).

**beauteous evil** A paradox – looking beautiful but inwardly evil – appearance and reality at an ironic level.

**empty trunks, o'er-flourished** Decorated boxes, but lacking substance (character).

**O prove true** Viola is praying that Sebastian – named by Antonio – is alive.

**couplet** Here perhaps a reference to Antonio's speech in rhyming verse.

**sage saws** Wise sayings.

**Yet living in my glass** i.e. because I see him whenever I look in the mirror. (Though they cannot be identical twins, being of different sexes, they still bear a strong likeness to each other.)

**'Slid** See note on *'Slight* p.40.

## Revision questions on Act III

**1** Show how the plot and the sub-plot come together in this Act.

**2** Examine the parts played by Sir Andrew *and* Malvolio in contributing to the comedy of this Act.

**3** Write an essay on the use of mistaken identity in any two scenes, saying what the consequences are.

**4** In what ways do you find the 'duel' plot funny? You should refer closely to the text in your answer.

**5** *Twelfth Night* is a romantic comedy. What aspects of this Act do you find unromantic or serious?

## Act IV Scene 1

The Clown has been sent to bring Viola to Olivia, and meets Sebastian, whom he naturally mistakes for her. Sebastian gives him money. Sir Andrew, entering with Sir Toby and Fabian, strikes Sebastian, who promptly beats him. Feste leaves hurriedly to tell Olivia what is happening, and Sir Toby and Sebastian draw their swords; Olivia enters, dismisses Sir Toby, and takes Sebastian to her house in the belief that she is taking Viola/Cesario. Sebastian appears to have fallen in love at first sight with Olivia.

### *Commentary*

This short scene emphasizes the consequences of mistaken identity, the arrival of Sebastian marking the dénouement of the action; the consequences are comic (the beating of Sir Andrew) and romantic (the delusion of Olivia and the response of Sebastian). Note the rhyming couplets which round off the scene on this romantic note.

**Go to** An expression of mild reproof.
**held out** Maintained.
**Nothing that is so, is so** A fine unconscious comment on the focus of the play – mistaken identity.
**vent** Release (but rather a high-sounding word).
**lubber** Fool.
**the world will prove a cockney** i.e. everyone will become affected in their behaviour
**ungird thy strangeness** Stop pretending that you don't know me.
**foolish Greek** Silly idiot.
**worse payment** i.e. strike him.
**open hand** Generous (and ready to slap)

**a good report ... fourteen years' purchase**  Make a good name for themselves ... and have to pay well for it.

**in some of your coats for twopence**  i.e. in your position (when Olivia sees that you are attacking 'Cesario').

**action for battery**  Summons for assault.

**my young soldier**  i.e. Sebastian.

**iron**  Sword.

**fleshed**  Used to bloodshed.

**malapert**  Impudent.

**Rudesby**  Ruffian.

**fair wisdom**  Judgement.

**uncivil and unjust extent**  Uncivilized and unlawful violence.

**Beshrew**  Curse.

**He started one poor heart ...**  He made my heart thump because of his (Sir Toby's) behaviour towards you. Note that the play on 'heart' echoes the Duke's play on the word in Act I Scene 1.

**What relish is in this?**  What does this all mean?

**Let fancy ... Lethe**  Let love overcome reason; let love make me forget to think (Sebastian is yielding himself up to the pleasure of the moment).

**would thou'dst**  I wish you would.


## Act IV Scene 2

Malvolio has now been locked up in a darkened room and Feste, aided by Maria, dresses up as 'Sir Topas the curate'. He is urged on by Sir Toby; when he talks to Malvolio, the latter asks him to go to Olivia. Feste reasons with him falsely in order to demonstrate his madness, and Sir Toby expresses the wish that they were 'well rid of this knavery', since he is now on the wrong side of Olivia. Malvolio begs for pen, ink and paper, but Feste assumes Sir Topas's voice in further torture of him. Feste ends by singing a promise to return.


### *Commentary*

The main dramatic effect of this scene is to extend further, and rather cruelly at that, the theme of deception and of mistaken identity. The alternation of Feste between Sir Topas's and his own voice appears to be orchestrated by Sir Toby, though the latter is clearly worried about the risk he is running. There is of course dramatic irony in the scene and much pathos; whatever we think of Malvolio, this joke has gone too far.

**Sir Topas**  There is some evidence that the precious stone topaz was thought to cure lunacy.

**dissemble**  Lie, pretend to be something you are not, and thus subserve the theme of the play.

**tall**  Impressive.

**the function**  i.e. the clerical role.

**lean**  Thin (one who goes without food in order to pursue his studies).

**good housekeeper**  i.e. generous in hospitality.

**as fairly . . . say**  As good as being known as.

**careful**  Conscientious.

**competitors**  Conspirators.

*Bonos dies*  Bad Latin for 'Good-day'.

**hermit of Prague**  Another of Feste's imaginary characters.

**King Gorboduc**  A legendary character in history, here used by Feste to impress his 'competitors'.

**'That that is, is'**  Continuing the mock vein of sounding wise and learned.

**hyperbolical**  Strong.

**barricadoes**  Strong barricades, they would not be 'transparent'. Feste is deliberately being paradoxical in order to undermine Malvolio.

**clerestories**  High windows.

**lustrous as ebony**  This is a continuation of the confusing nonsense.

**the Egyptians in their fog**  Exodus 10, 21–3: 'Let darkness, darkness so thick that it can be felt, cover the land of Egypt . . .'

**the trial**  The test.

**constant question**  Rational examination.

**Pythagoras**  Greek philosopher who taught that souls moved after death to the bodies of other creatures.

**grandam**  Grandmother.

**approve**  Support.

**allow of thy wits**  Testify that you are sane.

**dispossess**  Cast out.

**for all waters**  Able to do anything, take any part.

**conveniently delivered**  Easily released.

*Hey Robin*  By singing the clown resumes his real identity.

*perdie*  By God (from French *pardieu*).

**how fell you . . . five wits?**  How did you come to lose your senses?

**But as well?**  Only that well?

**propertied**  i.e. used.

**ministers**  Malvolio exaggerates – he means Sir Topas.

**face me out of my wits**  Convince me that I'm insane.

**Advise you**  Be careful.

**bibble babble**  Foolish talk.

**Maintain**  Have, hold.

**God buy you**  'God be with you', a greeting.

**shent**  Told off.

**Well-a-day**  If only.

**advantage thee more** Be of greater benefit to you.
**see his brains** Heavily sarcastic, implying that Malvolio hasn't got any.
**requite** Repay.
**the Old Vice** A conventional character in the medieval morality plays, he often raised a laugh by beating the Devil with a wooden dagger and trying to cut his long nails.
*goodman devil* Perhaps, as a parting shot, addressed to Malvolio.

## Act IV Scene 3

Sebastian, though somewhat concerned over Antonio, cannot get over Olivia's behaviour, which seems even more strange when she appears with a priest. She asks Sebastian to accompany her so that they can be betrothed; he agrees to do so.

### Commentary

This short scene merely emphasizes the romantic element of mistaken identity; it is crisp and to the point, and prepares us for the coming together of all the characters in their reality in Act V.

**was** Had been.
**credit** Report.
**my soul disputes well with my sense** My feelings and reason are in agreement.
**discourse** Reason.
**wrangle** Argue.
**deceivable** Misleading.
**chantry** Chapel, commonly attached to large houses.
**Plight** Pledge.
**Whiles** Until.
**come to note** Be revealed.
**What time** When.
**birth** Rank, status.
**fairly note** Bless, approve.

## Revision questions on Act IV

**1** Describe the part played by Feste in Act IV Scene 2.
**2** Consider the reactions of Sebastian in the two scenes in which he appears in this Act.
**3** Do you feel sorry for Malvolio or do you feel that he gets what he deserves? You should refer closely to the text in your answer.

**4** In what ways are the main themes of *Twelfth Night* emphasized in this Act?

## Act V Scene 1

This long scene brings to a conclusion all the main actions of the plot and sub-plots in the play. Feste and Fabian are discussing a letter, when Orsino enters – he has come to pay court to Olivia in person – and engages in a verbal flurry with Feste. The latter as ever wins it, but Orsino is impressed; they are dramatically interrupted by the arrival of Antonio and the officers, Viola pointing out that Antonio is the man who rescued her. Orsino recognizes Antonio for his past exploits, and demands an explanation; Antonio acknowledges his identity, and says that he rescued Sebastian from the sea and has followed him to the town, thus risking his own life. He says that for three months he and Viola (whom he mistakes for Sebastian) have been insepar-able. At this juncture Olivia enters, accuses Viola of being tardy, and rejects Orsino's love. Orsino, grown bitter, threatens to kill Viola, whom he too loves, rather than let Olivia have 'Cesario'.

Viola prepares to follow the Duke, but Olivia calls her 'hus-band' and summons the priest to testify that they are betrothed. This he does, and Orsino turns savagely on Viola; at this critical moment Sir Andrew enters, announcing that he and Sir Toby have been beaten by 'Cesario', Sir Toby following to confirm this. They leave to have their wounds treated, and Sebastian then appears; he tells Antonio not to fear, and Olivia and Orsino stand amazed at the spectacle of the twins they now see before them.

Viola and Sebastian are reunited, the Duke transfers his love to Viola (after all, Olivia is now married), and Feste re-enters with Malvolio's letter. Fabian is dispatched to get Malvolio, while the lovers arrange their wedding day at Olivia's house. Malvolio accuses Olivia of wronging him, but of course when Olivia sees the letter she points out to him that 'out of question, 'tis Maria's hand'. Fabian then confesses the plot against Malvolio, and says that Sir Toby has married Maria; Feste continues to bait Malvolio, who vows his revenge 'on the whole pack of you!' Feste's song ends the play.

## Commentary

The function of a concluding act – to round off everything – is exemplified by the speed of the action and the dramatic appearances that confuse and then resolve identities. Feste's word-play, the wit of the 'licensed fool', is notable in the early part of the scene in his exchanges with the Duke; it gives way immediately to the drama of Antonio's appearance and explanation – this in poetry of a moving and noble quality. Olivia's confusion over Viola, and the Duke's temporary bitterness are a climactic balance, the bitterness reflecting the darker side of this comedy, which is also shown in the treatment of Malvolio and the latter's own reactions later in this scene. The priest's testimony heightens the confusion and the tension, but the entrance of Sir Andrew is a comic spectacle – one sub-plot has misfired.

When Sebastian appears the fact of mistaken identity reaches its inevitable climax. The romantic comedy is thus romantically consummated, though perhaps we might cavil at the Duke's conveniently getting Viola after the self-indulgence of his 'love' for Olivia has occupied most of the main plot of the play; but balancing this happiness is the partial misfiring of the other sub-plot – the gulling of Malvolio – who is embittered by his treatment. There is genuine pathos in his letter to Olivia and his appearing before her, but despite the Duke's 'entreat him to a peace' we feel, with Olivia, that he has been 'most notoriously abused'. The Clown's final song, to an empty stage, is moving, poignant and uneven.

**his letter**  i.e. Malvolio's.
**to give a dog . . . my dog again**  This little exhange provides the
  opportunity for a set cant joke about the man who asked one favour in
  exchange for giving the Queen his favourite dog – that he might have
  his dog back again.
**trappings**  Hangers-on.
**abused**  Deceived.
**conclusions . . . affirmatives**  Two negatives make an affirmative in
  grammar, so here four lips make two kisses, although those kisses may
  have at first been refused.
**double-dealing**  Deception; paying out twice (Feste immediately hints
  that he would like more money).
**grace**  Virtue; with a pun on Orsino's title.
**flesh and blood**  Natural impulse, as opposed to 'grace'.
***Primo, secundo, tertio***  First, second, third.

**play** Throw at dice.

**'The third pays for all'** The equivalent of 'third time lucky'.

**triplex** Triple time, music for dancing.

**Saint Bennet** A well-known London church, Bennet being short for 'Benedict'.

**throw** Of the dice. See 'play' above.

**awake my bounty** Stimulate my generosity.

**lullaby to your bounty** i.e. may your generosity rest well (but reawaken when I return).

**Vulcan** Roman god who forged thunderbolts for Jove.

**baubling** Insignificant.

**unprizable** Hardly worth capturing.

**scathful grapple** Injurious struggle.

**bottom** Vessel. The term is still used in commerce today.

**That very envy . . . honour on him** All who resented his bravery and lost by it were compelled to praise and admire him.

**fraught** Cargo.

**Candy** Crete.

**desperate of shame and state** With reckless disregard for his situation.

**brabble** Brawl.

**Notable** Infamous.

**dear** Harmful (in terms of their losses).

**ground** We should use the plural 'grounds'.

**witchcraft** Further testimony to Viola's (and Sebastian's) attractiveness, which Olivia referred to as an 'enchantment'.

**redeem** Rescue.

**wrack** Castaway.

**dedication** Devoted service.

**pure** Only.

**twenty years' removed thing** i.e. as distant as someone I hadn't seen for that length of time.

**one would wink** i.e. in a moment.

**three months before** Not consistent with the time-scale elsewhere in the play, but Shakespeare was obviously not concerned with such details.

**but that he may not have** Orsino cannot have Olivia's love.

**Cesario . . .** Olivia doesn't know that this is not her husband; he in fact is crossing swords with Sir Toby.

**aught to the old tune** On the same old theme (of his love for her).

**fat and fulsome** Harsh and offensive.

**altars . . . off'rings . . . devotion** Note the religious language, an ironic comment on Orsino's self-indulgence.

**Even . . . become him** i.e. whatever you think fit.

**like to th'Egyptian thief** Thyamis, a robber chief, overcome by another band of robbers, tried to slay a captured maiden with whom he had fallen in love, rather than let her fall into their hands.

**a savage jealousy . . . nobly** Equivalent to 'Revenge tastes sweet'

**the instrument** i.e. Viola.

**screws** Forces out.

**marble-breasted** Hard-hearted.

**minion** Favourite.

**tender** Regard.

**Him will I tear . . . spite** I will take him from you who have allowed him to rule where I should rule.

**lamb** i.e. Viola.

**A raven's heart within a dove** i.e. the predatory heart of Olivia.

**jocund** Gladly.

**apt** Readily.

**do you rest** Satisfy you.

**by all mores** Beyond all compare.

**beguil'd** Misled.

**husband** i.e. Olivia and Sebastian are betrothed, but probably not yet formally married.

**strangle thy propriety** Deny your real self.

**Be that . . .** Acknowledge what you know yourself to be.

**as that thou fear'st** As he whom you fear (Orsino).

**newly pass'd** Recently occurred.

**joinder** Joining.

**sow'd a grizzle on thy case** i.e. put grey hairs on you (when you are older and more cunning).

**thine one trip** i.e. your cunning will lead to your own downfall.

**coxcomb** Head.

**incardinate** He means 'incarnate' but, ironically, the word is not inappropriate, since it sounds like 'incarnardine' (used in *Macbeth*) meaning 'to make red' (here with blood).

**'Ods lifelings** An oath (by God's life).

**set nothing by** Don't count.

**othergates** Otherwise.

**a passy measures pavin** An unsteady (because drunk) slowcoach.

**ass-head . . . gull** Injured, Sir Toby takes it out on Sir Andrew in this stream of insults.

**wit and safety** Care to safeguard myself.

**strange regard** This is not because of Sir Toby's injury, but because Sebastian is Viola's double.

**habit** Dress.

**A natural perspective** i.e. optical illusion produced by nature, and not by such devices as mirrors.

**Do I stand there?** Obviously Sebastian has just seen Viola, judging from what follows.

**deity** Divine attribute (of being in more than one place at one time).

**blind** Undiscriminating.

**If spirits . . . fright us** If souls can take on their mortal shapes then your ghost is causing us to fear.

**dimension** Human form.

**I did participate**  I've always had.
**goes even**  Coincides, fits in.
**record**  Remembrance.
**finished . . . mortal act**  Died.
**lets**  Is lacking.
**cohere and jump**  Agree completely.
**where**  At whose house.
**weeds**  Clothes.
**All the occurrence . . .**  All that has occurred.
**to her bias drew in that**  A metaphor from bowls meaning 'took your
  mistake into account and arrived at the right place by an indirect
  method'.
**to a maid and man**  i.e. she thought she was being betrothed to a man
  but would have been betrothed to a maid (Viola), but it may be just a
  reference to his own sexual innocence.
**the glass seems true**  i.e. what appears is reality.
**most happy wreck**  i.e. the good fortune of the shipwreck.
**Boy**  Superb ironic humour, since he knows now that 'Cesario' is a
  woman.
**over-swear**  Repeat.
**as doth . . . fire**  Just as truly as the sun brings in the dawn.
**action**  i.e. is legally held.
**durance**  Prison.
**enlarge**  Set at large, free.
**distract**  The past participle is now 'distraught'.
**extracting frenzy**  A madness which drove all other thoughts away.
**clearly**  Entirely.
**he holds Belzebub at the stave's end**  He is fighting to keep the Devil
  away.
**epistles are no gospels**  A double reference to (a) epistles as letters and
  (b) religious epistles and gospels, not necessarily the same or true, as
  indeed one cannot accept that Malvolio's 'epistle' would be 'gospel'
  (truth).
**skills**  Matters.
**delivers**  Repeats the words of, like an actor.
*vox*  The correct or right tone of voice.
**read . . . read thus**  i.e. because he is mad (I have to read the way I do –
  Feste is giving a performance by simulating a madman's voice).
**perpend**  Consider (typical of the Clown's choice of inflated words).
*semblance*  Appearance.
**I leave my duty a little unthought of**  I step a little outside my usual
  respectful limits.
**This savours not . . .**  This doesn't sound much like . . .
**crown th' alliance on't**  See the double marriage ceremony.
**proper**  Own.
**quits**  Frees.
**mettle**  Nature.

**soft and tender** Genteel.
**from it** i.e. in a different way.
**the modesty of honour** The way of right conduct.
**clear lights** Obvious signals.
**lighter people** Lesser in status and behaviour.
**geck** Dupe.
**character** Style of handwriting.
**presuppos'd** Already hinted at.
**This practice hath . . .** This plot has been most cruelly set against you
**Taint the condition** Spoil the atmosphere.
**stubborn and uncourteous parts** Inflexible and rude behaviour.
**conceiv'd** Noticed.
**importance** Insistence.
**sportful** Playful.
**pluck on** Call for.
**Alas, poor fool . . .** Almost certainly addressed kindly to Malvolio, but
  it could mean that Feste has been tricked into taking part in the plot
  against Malvolio.
**thrown** Changed from 'thrust' in the letter, a subtle variant which
  shows the depth at which Shakespeare worked – Feste uses it with full
  disrespect.
**golden time convents** i.e. summoned at the best possible time.
**fancy's queen** Ruler of his heart.
*A foolish thing* i.e. a naughty child.
*'Gainst knaves and thieves . . .* i.e. I found people against me (the
  spoiled child has grown up into a knave and thief).
*unto my beds . . . drunken heads* Since the song is tracing the process
  from childhood to old age, this looks as if it means 'when I became old
  I (or we) went to bed drunk nightly'.


## Revision questions on Act V

**1** Show clearly, by close reference to the text, how the various
aspects of mistaken identity are resolved in this Act.

**2** Do you find the ending of the play satisfactory? You might
refer to the reactions of the Duke and the part played by Malvolio in this long scene.

**3** In what way is Feste's song a comment on the main themes of
the play?

**4** 'Romantic rather than humorous.' How far does this description fit Act V?

**5** Compare and contrast any *two* speeches in this act.

**6** In what ways is the role of Antonio important in the final
unravelling of the plot?

# General questions

1 'All our interest centres on Viola'. Discuss.

*Notes for an answer:* (a) Viola the central and most sympathetic character in the play. (b) General statement of her qualities. These might include: spirit in response to adversity of ship-wreck and (supposed) loss of brother; trust and openness (re the sea captain); impressionability (falls in love with Orsino); intelligence (many examples); wit (many examples); pathos of her situation re Orsino and embarrassment of her situation (re Olivia). Linked to these, complications of mistaken identity or disguise, quality of her loyalty; imagination ('Build me a willow cabin . . .'), vulnerability (the mock duel). Include any other points which make her the centre of the reader's interest.

THEN give points which might possibly make our interest shift from her: (a) the humour of the sub-plot (Sir Toby, Maria, Sir Andrew, the gulling of Malvolio); (b) our interest in Malvolio and his changed situation; (c) the general mistaken identity scenes; (d) the speed of the action of the play (something is always happening).

Conclude with *brief* summary of reasons why you think Viola is central or why you think other elements of the play are of greater interest.

2 Which character do you think is the main connecting link between the main plot and the sub-plot? By close reference to the play, examine the role of this character in some detail.

3 Write an essay on the subject of mistaken identity in the play *without* including Viola as Cesario.

4 Define and illustrate the various means employed by Shakespeare to provide humour in *Twelfth Night*.

5 Discuss and illustrate from various scenes Viola's (a) common sense, (b) humour, and (c) the pathos of her situation.

6 Compare and contrast the characters of Viola and Olivia as young women in love.

7 Describe in some detail the sub-plot that leads to the gulling of Malvolio and indicate its main results.

**8** 'Malvolio gets what he deserves.' Discuss.

**9** Compare and contrast Sir Toby Belch and Sir Andrew Aguecheek.

**10** Write an essay on Shakespeare's use of song in *Twelfth Night*.

**11** What do you learn of Elizabethan life and leisure from *Twelfth Night*? You should refer closely to the text and quote in support of your answer.

**12** Write an essay on the role and actions of Feste.

**13** 'We ought not to like this drunken reveller, but we all do.' How far would you agree with this estimate of Sir Toby Belch?

**14** Indicate the role played by Fabian in *Twelfth Night*.

**15** Orsino has been called a completely unsympathetic character. How far would you agree or disagree with this statement?

**16** Give three or four examples of dramatic irony from the play and explain fully what effect they have on the audience and the reader.

**17** Examine in some detail the use of verse and prose in *Twelfth Night*.

**18** Who is the greater fool, Malvolio or Sir Andrew? Give reasons for your answer.

**19** In what ways are Sebastian and Antonio important to our appreciation of *Twelfth Night*?

**20** Consider the use of *either* (a) word-play (b) imagery (c) rhymed verse (d) the soliloquy (e) letters in *Twelfth Night*.

# Shakespeare's art in *Twelfth Night*
## The characters

### Viola

> I'll do my best
> To woo your lady: yet a barful strife!
> Whoe'er I woo, myself would be his wife.

Hazlitt has rightly observed that 'The great and secret charm of *Twelfth Night* is the character of Viola.' She is one of the most appealing of Shakespeare's heroines, her initial situation arousing compassion and admiration, She is practical and courageous enough to determine on a course of action and carry it through. Her grief for the brother she thinks she has lost is soon translated into action, and she is not so overcome as to bemoan her or her brother's fate. Early in the play we are made aware of her vivacity and her natural, feminine interest in Orsino before she meets him. 'He was a bachelor then' is an unconsciously ironic observation on what she wishes him to remain – for her sake – when she does meet him. And her trust in the captain and her initiative in disguising herself and going to Orsino's court are winning qualities. Viola, without being smug, knows that she has talents that can be put to good advantage: 'for I can sing,/And speak to him in many sorts of music' (I, 2.), which is again an unconscious anticipation of Orsino's needs (remember the importance of music to him and in the play as a whole).

Orsino is in love with love, Viola loves; her emotions are real, spontaneous, warm. We see her try to dissuade the Duke from sending her to court Olivia on his behalf, but she undertakes it out of loyalty to him and despite the inward suffering it occasions her, as we see from the quotation at the head of this section – 'myself would be his wife'. And right through to the unravellings of Act V we are aware of Viola's love and marvel at the way she sustains herself in emotional adversity. Courting Olivia for Orsino, she has the wit to mock the whole process of such second-hand love by adopting a pompously mock-heroic tone, brilliantly in keeping with the affectations of love rather than its reality ('Most radiant, exquisite, and unmatchable beauty . . .'), laughing at her own role at the same time ('I have taken great pains to con it').

Viola's send-up of her own position, and of Orsino's and Olivia's is reinforced by a natural and spontaneous ability to be funny, and a wonderful variety of tone, which takes in the pompous ('I bring no overture of war, no taxation of homage') and the epigrammatic ('to your ears, divinity; to any other's, profanation'). At first ironic about Olivia's beauty, she is generous in her praise of it, even to the point of urging Orsino's suit with some passion, a passion which is a sublimation of her own. And soon she is able to express that passion in some of the finest poetry of the play, as she identifies herself with Orsino's supposed love in the lyrical expression of her own. It is a superbly romantic but none the less real focus. She tells Olivia she would:

Make me a willow cabin at your gate,
And call upon my soul within the house;
Write loyal cantons of contemned love,
And sing them loud even in the dead of night;
Halloo your name to the reverberate hills,
And make the babbling gossip of the air
Cry out 'Olivia!' (I,5)

It is no wonder that Olivia responds, for Viola's hyperbole is infused with feeling.

Viola has pride, refusing Olivia's money, and is outspoken too, calling her 'fair cruelty' as she carries back her rejection to Orsino. But when Malvolio follows her to return the ring, she is quick to see that Olivia has been indiscreet, and covers that by a ready admission that the ring is her own ('She took the ring of me'). When Malvolio has gone she ponders on Olivia's motive, acknowledging to herself and the audience that 'I left no ring with her'. Now Viola's first reaction is a generous one, her second a thoughtful and keen evaluation of what has really happened, namely that Olivia has fallen in love with her. She responds to Orsino's overbearing assertion of man's greater capacity to love with humility and discipline, her own created abstraction of 'Patience on a monument' being her self-control and determination to continue 'Smiling at grief', a nobler expression of love and acceptance than Orsino's exaggeration of passion – he feels what he thinks he should feel. Viola's 'I am all the daughters of my father's house,/And all the brothers too' (II, 4) is a moving reminder that she still feels that Sebastian is dead, here epigrammatically expressed and totally lacking Olivia's advertised self-indulgence in grief.

Viola's exchange with Feste at the beginning of Act III reveals further facets of her character; her capacity for rational argument, for playing on words as professionally as Feste, for enjoyment of the verbal duel (we are soon to see how she will shun the physical one) is complemented by a good-humoured and tolerant attitude. Her frankness and honesty, which she is forced to hide, are never far from the surface; faced with Olivia's love for herself, she expresses her compassion for her but tellingly observes, 'That you do think you are not what you are'. This double-edged comment, defining Olivia's being in love with love – and being in love with a woman though she does not know it – shows Viola telling the truth in spite of her position.

The projected duel with Sir Andrew places Viola in an embarrassing, worrying position. This draws out all the sympathy of the audience, not because she need fear Sir Andrew but because she does. Her admission that 'I am one that had rather go with sir priest than sir knight' reveals her feminine sensibility, while her 'A little thing would make me tell them how much I lack of a man' shows her witty response – there is sexual innuendo here – even in adversity. She does draw her sword, and we feel that this is courageous.

Resilient though she is, Viola is bewildered by Antonio's request for his money. Even then, she asserts her moral belief in no uncertain terms, saying

I hate ingratitude more in a man
Than lying, vainness, babbling drunkenness,
Or any taint of vice whose strong corruption
Inhabits our frail blood (III, 4)

When we note that she has just recovered from the near duel and Antonio's demand, it is a remarkable and sincere response to a situation with which she cannot cope – though she has just borne witness to her own generosity by offering Antonio what she can.

Excited and moved by the mention of Sebastian's name, Viola stores her hopeful joy in secret while the events of Act IV ensure the climactic revelations of Act V, in which she is to experience both bewilderment and happiness. Her love for the Duke makes her both subservient and suffering, loyal and anguished; she is prepared to die for him (though we feel this is in keeping with the exaggerated actions of the Duke) and turns angrily on Olivia who seeks to keep her there, saying 'Who does beguile you? Who does do you wrong?'. Spirit there has always been, but this spark shows the extreme tension she is under. Events overtake her; she can hardly get a word in and, with the arrival of Sebastian, is almost too moved to do so anyway. Then her practicality asserts itself once more, and in order to authenticate beyond doubt her own identity she offers to take Sebastian to the sea captain who saved her. Viola says no more; her presence has been enough to provide warmth, pathos, sympathy, humour, wit.

Above all it is her sincerity that makes Viola stand out, and this is seen in contrast to Orsino's love of love and Olivia's self-indulgence. She never loses her self-respect. The somewhat contrived ending makes us a little sorry for Viola; we cannot applaud her subservience to Orsino (although it is informed with passion) for we feel that she deserves better. She remains the most lovable of Shakespeare's heroines, lacking the acid of Beatrice but perhaps closest to Rosalind in spirit. And it is this spirit, intelligence, tenderness and wit, together with the pathos of her position, that keeps her constantly before us in sympathetic immediacy.


## Orsino

There is no woman's sides
Can bide the beating of so strong a passion
As love doth give my heart;

The above quotation is definitive of Orsino's love, but it is largely self-love and love of the idea of being in love which motivates him. His melancholy self-indulgence in rejection, with musical accompaniment from time to time as fitting index to his mood, shows him to be largely indolent. He is spoken of as being virtuous and noble and 'in dimension and the shape of nature/A gracious person', but his words are affected and exaggerated, as when he seizes on the word 'hart' in the first scene and elaborates upon its particularity to himself. He luxuriates emotionally and physically: 'Away before me to sweet beds of flowers!/Love-thoughts lie rich when canopied with bowers.' (I, 1).The arrival of Viola as Cesario heightens his resolve to court Olivia, but it is courtship at second hand, and although we would like to think that this is lack of confidence it smacks more directly of indolence.

Admittedly Orsino does display a certain consciousness of his age and the greater attractions that youth can present when he says: 'She will attend it better in thy youth, /Than in a nuncio's of more grave aspect.' (I, 4). But there is foolishness in this too, and poor Viola reaps the results; Olivia does indeed 'attend it better' by falling in love with Viola. He appears older by some years than Viola, referring disparagingly to 'these most brisk and giddy-paced times'. The lecture he gives Viola on love shows a mind closed to experience but obsessed by 'the constant image of the creature/That is belov'd'. We should note his use of the word 'image', a poor substitute for 'reality'. He has some insight, though, seeing into Viola's feelings of love without in any way associating them with himself. Yet he is curiously inconsistent, saying that men's love is more unreliable than women's (II, 4) and later in the same scene observing:

> Make no compare
> Between that love a woman can bear me
> And that I owe Olivia.

Perhaps — and this would be very subtle characterization — Shakespeare intends the Duke to be inconsistent in order to show the superficiality of his love and to prepare the way for his sudden greatest change — his turning towards Viola and transferring his 'love' to her when he discovers that Olivia is betrothed to Sebastian. His 'love' for Olivia is forgotten, the transference is quickly made, and he urges Viola to 'let me see thee in thy woman's weeds'. Orsino is not deeply drawn, but his selfish, moody, changeable nature and his constant talking about his own love make him unequal to Viola, who never told hers. He is an unheroic, patronizing egoist.

## Olivia

> How now?
> Even so quickly may one catch the plague?

Olivia is subject to melancholy, but not quite in the same way as Orsino. Before we meet her we are told that she is mourning the death of her brother, whom 'she would keep fresh/And lasting in her sad remembrance'. Sir Toby deplores her morbidness, yet her first exchanges with Feste and, above all, her reception of and response to Viola, show that her grief in reality sits lightly upon her. Verbally outmanoeuvred by Feste she invites Malvolio's comments, and swiftly puts the latter down for his self-love, rightly saying that 'There is no slander in an allowed fool, though he do nothing but rail.' This admirable sense of perspective is quickly undermined, but not before she has sparred again with Feste and dispatched Malvolio to get rid of Orsino's messenger, Viola. Malvolio's description of Viola as 'very well-favoured' intrigues Olivia who, setting her grief aside, with feminine inquisitiveness admits Viola to her presence. Behind the mourning veil she is able to conceal her reactions.

Not only is Olivia intrigued, she is impressionable enough and vulnerable enough to try to protect herself by irony, but it is to no avail; she falls in love at first sight. The melancholy, perhaps a combination of self-indulgence or even a shield against Orsino's overtures, is gone. She asks Maria and her attendants to leave, and what may be described as a witty flirtation with Viola takes place. The conceit that she 'will give out divers schedules of my beauty' is brilliantly sustained and reveals the quality of her mind – she is intelligent and witty with a kind of dry humour. She follows this with a generous recognition of Orsino's qualities (though they cannot move her to love). Although she wants Viola to return, and cunningly, at first unashamedly, sends the ring after her, it is when she is left alone after this first meeting that the full acknowledgement is made:

Methinks I feel this youth's perfections
With an invisible and subtle stealth
To creep in at mine eyes. (Act I Scene 5)

She even reveals to Malvolio, though inadvertently, the suddenness of her change ('If that the youth will come this way tomorrow') and then resigns herself to fate.

Viola's next visit (Act III Scene 1) finds Olivia outwardly responsive and commendably honest; she admits sending the ring after Viola following 'the last enchantment you did here'. She even manages to laugh at her own love, assuring Viola 'Be not afraid, good youth, I will not have you', though we suspect that this is a cover for her own emotion. Soon comes the outright confession of her love, and that confession is not without dignity and self-recognition:

I love thee so, that maugre all thy pride,
Nor wit nor reason can my passion hide.

Do not extort thy reasons from this clause,
For that I woo, though therefore hast no cause;
But rather reason thus with reason fetter:
Love sought is good, but given unsought is better.

We share Viola's pity for her, since such love is misplaced for (unbeknown to her) one of her own sex, but we cannot help but admire the open expression of it. So desperate is she for Viola's company that she begs her to come again, saying she may even be moved 'to like his love' (Orsino's). This shows how human Olivia is, and how overcome she is by her feelings.

Thinking that the 'sad and civil' behaviour of Malvolio will suit with her mood, Olivia sends for her steward, not realizing how he has been gulled. She is bewildered but compassionate, ordering that Malvolio be cared for (this is perversely interpreted by Sir Toby, Fabian and Maria) and showing how much she values him. After Sebastian appears on the scene she moves swiftly to their betrothal, but perhaps with a qualm of conscience that she has ceased to mourn for her brother. Her reliance on 'fate' has worked out well though she hopes that 'the heavens' will look favourably on her action. With the revelations of Act V Olivia is as bewildered as anyone, and 'beguiled' too, but acts nobly and with dignity, not only when the identities are resolved, but in relation to Malvolio too: she later observes of him, 'He hath been most notoriously abused.' Olivia has more control over her household than she has over herself, but she is generous too, and she shows no indignation at Malvolio's fancying that she could be in love with him.

Olivia is susceptible, witty, sympathetic, honest, and must not be undervalued. Her feelings in interaction with Viola – and Malvolio – are real. Like Viola, she has spirit; she is an engaging character, with more depth than she is sometimes given credit for.


## Sebastian

> My kind Antonio,
> I can no other answer make, but thanks,
> And thanks, and ever thanks

Sebastian is a good character, existing more as a plot device and balance than as an individual. He is an affectionate brother, mourning the supposed loss of Viola, and more than grateful as we see from the above quotation, to Antonio for saving him and caring for him. He gives us the details of his birth and of his sister, does not wish to involve Antonio in further trouble and decides to explore the town by himself. He is independent and a man of action, drawing his sword upon Sir Toby and Sir Andrew together and thus showing his courage. Just as Orsino is quick to turn to Viola at the end, so Sebastian accepts what Olivia offers him – her love – for he has apparently fallen in love at first sight too. He seems to be a character of plain common sense, grateful, making quick decisions, and perhaps impetuous: witness his response to Sir Toby and to Olivia.

## Antonio

If you will not murder me for my love, let me be your servant.

Antonio represents loyalty in friendship. Having saved Sebastian he becomes devoted to him, so much so that he fears for his safety and wishes to accompany him wherever he goes. We sense something possessive and unhealthy in that love, but admire his courage in following Sebastian into an area where he knows his own life is at risk – because of a previous sea-fight against Orsino's galleys. He goes to arrange accommodation for Sebastian and himself and, in giving Sebastian his purse, shows his generosity. Viola's denial of him provides a poignant moment since loyalty is one of the themes of the play. His reaction to what he considers betrayal ('O how vile an idol proves this god!') is moving in its forthrightness and anguish. He is rewarded by Sebastian's unequivocal assertion of his feelings in Act V Scene 1:

Antonio! O my dear Antonio,
How have the hours rack'd and tortur'd me,
Since I have lost thee!

## Malvolio

I leave my duty a little unthought of, and
speak out of my injury.

Malvolio is perhaps the most interesting character in *Twelfth Night*, and critical opinion is still divided over whether he merits his fate or whether he is 'most notoriously abused'. In a romantic comedy his is the rounded but somewhat dark character, and his gulling smacks of dark comedy rather than the more conventional variety. He is a competent and respected steward for Olivia, who would 'not have him miscarry for the half of my dowry'. Olivia obviously depends on him; she sends him to encounter Viola at the gate, and gives him leave to deal with the matter as he wishes. There is something pathetic even this early in the play when Malvolio reports back his lack of success in curbing Viola's wish for admission. It mirrors his lack of success with Sir Toby and the servants, for he is pompous, condescending, a figure of fun in his self-conceit, provoking Maria to the gulling and provoking Fabian to join it in revenge for having been reported for bear-baiting.

Malvolio is the Puritan spoil-sport who sets himself in opposition to the 'cakes and ale' activity of the household. His inflated opinion of himself and his status is seen on a number of occasions, the first being his denigration of Feste to Olivia who, though she values Malvolio, accuses him of being 'sick of self-love' and of taking things too seriously. But one wonders if she is right. If Malvolio fails through moral vanity, then what are we to make of Sir Toby and Maria? Admittedly, Malvolio cuts a comic figure even before the gulling and we can feel little sympathy for his complacency. But he has responsibilities, and the attitude of the household is obstructive to him. In a sense we understand why he attacks Sir Toby and why he enjoys attacking him – it is an outlet for his own frustration and failure. He is high-handed, he is a tale-bearer, he inevitably strikes a sour note:

> She returns this ring to you, Sir: you might have saved me my pains, to have taken it away yourself . . . If it be worth stooping for, there it lies in your eye; if not, be it his that finds it. (Act II Scene 2)

A 'churlish messenger' indeed, but it would be superficial to ignore the circumstances; the deception is Olivia's, which Malvolio cannot know, and moreover 'Orsino's embassy' as conducted by Viola has disturbed Olivia's mourning, which Malvolio would surely be required to guard.

Malvolio lacks humour, is unable to see even a verbal joke (he calls the Clown a 'barren rascal'). He has a touch of the hypocrite, abandoning his conscientious Puritanical scruples and dressing as 'Olivia' would have him dress, in 'yellow stockings' which are 'cross-gartered'. There is little doubt that Maria's letter finds him able to indulge those things he has repressed, from outward show of his inward vanity to thoughts above his station in the person of Olivia. The letter gives us an insight into his thoughts; it shows the ponderous and slow-churning responses of a man eaten up by his own vanity and thus able to interpret the enigmas and acrostics to his own self-satisfaction. Yet there is something pathetic in his delusion, and some justification in his 'Go hang yourselves all: you are idle, shallow things, I am not of your element.' Even if we appreciate the fun, we could hardly ask for a better description of that irresponsible group.

The further gulling of Malvolio in the darkened room with the Clown disguised as 'Sir Topas' shows, as Sir Toby is later to admit, that the joke has gone too far; 'They have laid me here in hideous darkness ... I am no more mad than you are'. Above all there is the honesty which makes Malvolio say (in reply to the Clown's question on Pythagoras and the transmigration of souls) 'I think nobly of the soul, and no way approve his opinion'. This enlarges our sympathies. Certainly Malvolio is not of their 'element'; he is reduced through this mental and emotional torture to begging Feste for ink and paper. The pathos of his situation, the humiliation he suffers when brought before everybody, is enough to call forth our sympathy and to reject Fabian's explanation that the plot was undertaken more in 'laughter' than 'revenge', (a convenient emphasis to ingratiate himself with Olivia now that Maria and Sir Toby have left him, with the 'allowed fool', to face the music.) Despite all the unattractive facets of Malvolio's character and personality, he exemplifies the quality of Shakespeare's characterization. He is raised into sympathy through suffering, provided with human stature through the loss of his beloved status. He has been wounded where for him it would hurt most – in his vanity. We do not know whether he has learned a hard lesson. It doesn't matter; we have seen him duped and shared his suffering, as we see and share in life. That, in fact, is the convincing reality of Malvolio.

## Sir Toby

I am sure care's an enemy to life.

There is a tendency to regard Sir Toby as a lovable rogue, a kind of lightweight Falstaff who staggers through the scenes of *Twelfth Night* echoing his own aptly-chosen name. There is something in this but there is, as so often with Shakespeare, more to it; Sir Toby is a drunken reveller who is intent always on enjoyment, generally at everyone else's expense and more particularly at Sir Andrew's. The latter is fleeced by Sir Toby, who succeeds in keeping up his pretensions to Olivia's hand. Far from being lightweight, Sir Toby is an accomplished liar, even in his cups; witness his exaggerations about Sir Andrew's ability to speak 'three or four languages word for word without book'. He is witty, sometimes deliberately, sometimes in the slurred manner of the drunkard; he is boisterous and satirical, mocking Sir Andrew to his face, though of course the latter does not understand it. He is also bawdy, impetuous and hot-headed. He delights in stirring up mischief or trouble, has a sense of rank (without breeding) which makes him abuse Malvolio for his anticipated condescension, yet spends his time with the servants since they meet his requirements of liveliness and sociability.

When we think of his escapades early in the play we should perhaps remember that Olivia is in mourning; when we think of them later in the play we should remember that he tries to initiate a duel and clears off when he suspects that the plot against Malvolio has somewhat backfired. He is rude and ill-bred, telling Malvolio to 'Sneck up!' and to 'rub your chain with crumbs'. He is not as intelligent as Maria, but he generously acknowledges the quality of her 'device' to humiliate Malvolio. He also rests complacently in the idea that Maria adores him but watching Malvolio preening himself, is moved to say 'Shall this fellow live?'. After the success of the gulling, he says that he 'could marry this wench for this device', a tribute indeed but small basis for marriage, unless he regards that too as yet another practical joke in the series.

In fact the next practical joke – the duping of Sir Andrew and Viola into a duel – is initiated by Sir Toby, whose language often smacks of blood-sports in the field. He follows this by having 'care' for Malvolio, (a distortion of Olivia's instructions) 'we'll have him in a dark room and bound'. Admittedly he says that when they are tired of it they will have mercy on him, but he is next concerned to establish Sir Andrew's fearsome reputation with Viola. It almost works, and it is almost as sick as the trick on Malvolio. We note too that Sir Toby expects some profit from it, namely Sir Andrew's horse. He shows courage when confronted by Antonio, and affects to – or does – despise Viola for denying

Antonio. He continues to promote the baiting of Malvolio in the dark room, and in fact directs Feste's performance, getting him to change from Sir Topas to his own voice in order to compound the deception. He gets what he deserves when he is beaten by Sebastian, though earlier he has acknowledged that he has gone too far in the duping of Malvolio, and that he will not regain favour with Olivia. His marriage to Maria is almost one of necessity; there is nowhere left for him to go. We may enjoy him but we cannot sympathize with him. He has rank and the security of being Olivia's uncle; he abuses both. He is a rogue.

## Sir Andrew

I knew 'twas I, for many do call me fool.

Sir Andrew's remark above is definitive of himself; he is a fool. His is the chameleon personality of imbecility, his country simplicity making him the dupe of Sir Toby, who unscrupulously fleeces him and keeps him hanging on as a potential courtier of Olivia. Sir Andrew follows Sir Toby implicitly, echoing his words and his actions; he never once suspects that he is being cheated or used. Maria too plays with him, verbally and physically, in Act I Scene 3. He never once understands Sir Toby's satirical fun at his expense. Just occasionally, he utters a truth which he would not recognize himself, as when he replies to Sir Toby's 'Does not our life consist of the four elements?', 'I think rather consists of eating and drinking.' When he and Sir Toby have absorbed Maria's plan, Sir Andrew pathetically remarks, 'I was adored once too', an indication that he feels the need to be loved. Watching Malvolio strut, Sir Andrew refers to him as 'Jezebel', sufficient indication of his ignorance and at the same time his need to assert himself as strongly as his companions and thus be accepted by them. He recognizes Malvolio's description of himself without in any way realizing its significance – that he is a fool because he is being robbed and used with his eyes, (for all that they can see) open. It is significant that as Malvolio traces the false clues of the letter Sir Andrew is silent – such verbal mysteries are beyond his powers of comprehension. But when Sir Toby says that he could marry Maria for her scheme, Sir Andrew as ever provides his inappropriate echo – 'So could I too'. He has his simple moments of envy, as when he hears Viola's courtier-like invocation to Olivia – 'the heavens rair odours on you' – and realizes the inadequacy of his own vocabulary. He is so upset as to wish to leave forthwith, but Sir Toby and Fabian easily talk him out of it.

He allows himself to be persuaded to write a challenge to Viola; his letter is as ridiculous as Maria's but of course completely lacking her consummate art. It ranges between cowardice and nonsense, contradiction and spurious invective. Faced with the duel, he offers his horse to get out of it; but when Sir Toby says that Viola is a coward, Sir Andrew replies : 'Slid, I'll after him again, and beat him'. When he and Sir Toby are beaten by Sebastian, he is still able to assert that Sir Toby would have 'tickled you othergates' if he had not been drinking. Naive, silly, pathetic, unconsciously humorous throughout, Sir Andrew is a brilliant comic creation; he too is 'notoriously abused', and perhaps it would be right to describe him as the natural fool in a play where the allowed fool has all the natural ability.

## Maria

I know this letter will make a contemplative idiot of him

We first meet Maria in Act I Scene 3, where she is trying to persuade Sir Toby to come in earlier at night and to behave himself. Maria is initially a peacemaker, but soon a mischief-maker. She has a sharp tongue and sharp eyes; she tells Sir Toby how he is getting into Olivia's bad graces, and defines Sir Andrew's foolishness and cowardice. Yet almost in sudden and unvoiced conspiracy with Sir Toby she satirizes Sir Andrew to his face by jesting on 'hand', 'thought' 'dry' and 'barren'. She next engages in a bout of word-play with Feste, and this is followed by her reception of Viola when the latter has come to court Olivia. Taking her mistress's mood she says 'Will you hoist sail, sir? Here lies your way.' But her sharpness, effective enough with others, is not equal to Viola's resilience, and she retires when Olivia wishes to be alone with Viola.

Maria devises the plan to gull Malvolio. This shows her cleverness, her shrewdness, her practical ability, the quality of her imagination; it also shows her ability to read character; her appraisal of Malvolio is worth noting:

. . . a time-pleaser, an affectioned ass, that cons state without book, and utters it by great swarths: the best persuaded of himself, so crammed (as he thinks) with excellencies, that it is his grounds of faith that all that look on him love him: and on that vice in him will my revenge find notable cause to work. (Act II Scene 3)

She is right, intelligent, spirited, and we wonder if at the back of her mind there is the thought that this 'device' may make her Lady Belch, as indeed it does. But if Maria is cunning here, she is also somewhat two-faced, for she can be prim and proper as Olivia's lady's-maid, yet enjoy this joke and the company of the revellers; just as Feste is 'for all waters' so is Maria, adapting herself to the various company she keeps. Her language is vivid and apt — 'Here comes the trout that must be caught with tickling,' she says as Malvolio prepares to become the 'contemplative idiot' she is intent on making him. Her forgery is superb, yet she does not witness the effects of it. Told of them by Sir Toby and his echo Sir Andrew, she urges them on to mark the effects when Malvolio comes before Olivia. She even feels that 'my lady will strike him', but she is wrong; she prepares Olivia for Malvolio's madness, and puts on a bold act of reproving him, saying 'Why appear you with this ridiculous boldness before my lady?'. Maria is a positive character; the maker of plots, ingenious, entertaining, sharp, essentially practical.

### Feste, the Clown (Latin 'festus'=cheerful, gay)

He must observe their mood on whom he jests,
The quality of persons, and the time;
................................................................
This is a practice
As full of labour as a wise man's art.

Feste is central to one of the main dramatic effects of *Twelfth Night*; I refer to word-play, argument, clever reasoning which makes entertainment. Feste is a professional fool, an 'allowed' fool and, as Olivia says, there is no 'slander' in him. He engages in word-play with everybody, sings the songs appropriate to the current mood — including the song that is an effective epilogue to the play — and enjoys participating in the revenge on Malvolio, for the latter has attempted to put him down. Like Maria, he has great insight into character, and his comments are shrewd — as shrewd as his verbal dexterity, which means that he can virtually out-argue anybody. By nature he is 'for all waters', and he certainly picks up as many tips as he can. He joins the revellers, and the only time he shows a streak of bitterness is when he is speaking of Malvolvio or mocking him; for him the imprisoning of Malvolio ensures that 'the whirligig of time brings in his revenges'.

Clever and good-humoured, Feste is certainly strongly in favour of practical jokes, but there is also an element of the opportunist in his character, e.g. hastening off to tell Olivia when Sir Toby and Sir Andrew engage with Sebastian in mistake for Viola. Feste is absent for some time at Orsino's, and this is never satisfactorily explained. His ingenious wit covers a void in his character; words cannot replace reality. The Clown has always to be acting; it is his profession. He lives by wit, but appears to have no life beyond it, and this provides a pathos which is, by a masterly stroke of irony, present in each of the songs he sings.

## Fabian

I will not give my part of this sport for a pension of thousands to be paid from the Sophy.

Fabian delights in sport, being in trouble with a 'bear-baiting here' about which Malvolio has told Olivia. He enters the play at the time of the gulling of Malvolio, whom he detests as much as the others do, and he takes part in this and in the hoaxing of Sir Andrew. He conspires with Sir Toby to convince Sir Andrew that Olivia really loves him and thus stirs him up to the challenge; at the same time he keeps up a running commentary on the inadequacy of that challenge. He tells Viola that Sir Andrew is 'the most skilful, bloody, and fatal opposite that you could have found in any part of Illyria'. He also says he will try to make peace on her account, and just as he and Toby have got them to the duel the officers appear with Antonio.

Fabian is not involved in the fight with Sebastian or with the imprisoning of Malvolio in the dark room, but he is present in the last act and tells Olivia how Malvolio came to be baited and also that Sir Toby has married Maria. Fabian seems merely to contribute to the gullings of the two sub-plots; he certainly has intelligence and wit and also gets his revenge on Malvolio, but he seems to want to avoid trouble, hence his final words to Olivia and his staying clear of getting a 'bloody coxcomb'.

## Minor characters

The minor characters are functional. The sea-captain who befriends and helps to save Viola represents goodness without complexity; his appearance is consonant with his feelings and his character. The priest exists to provide testimony to Olivia's betrothal, Curio and Valentine merely attend the Duke, the first registering his melancholy and the second Viola's advancement in his favours. Similarly, the officers who arrest Antonio merely exist as confirmation of his earlier story.

# Structure and style

## Structure
### 1 *Basic contrasts*

As we have seen, the main plot in *Twelfth Night* concerns Olivia, Viola, Orsino and Sebastian. Set in contrast to this, but interacting with it, are the revellings and plottings of Sir Toby and Maria, the culmination being the gulling and then the imprisonment of Malvolio, and finally the gulling and bewilderment of poor Sir Andrew. Contrast is of the essence in this play; it binds the structure with an adhesive of comparison and parallel. Thus Orsino is suitor to Olivia, and Sir Andrew a potential if ridiculous suitor to her as well. Orsino expends his leisure in music and the indulgence of melancholy love, Olivia spends hers in the indulgence of sentimental and melancholy grief. By contrast, Olivia falls quickly in love (with Viola/Cesario), as does Viola (with Orsino); Viola's quickness enables her to assume male disguise and become Cesario, while Sebastian with like speed adjusts to the advances of Olivia and agrees to become betrothed to her. After his initial anger, Orsino too reacts quickly, transferring his affections to the 'Boy' who will be his 'Fancy's queen'.

The sub-plot concerning Malvolio exhibits a beautifully comparable pace of action; the idea for the duping of Malvolio originates with the quick-witted Maria, who breaks it to Sir Toby and the virtually uncomprehending Sir Andrew (Act II, Scene 3), sees it implemented (Act II, Scene 5) and reaps the fulfilment of it in the same scene via the watchers in the box-tree. There is almost a double epilogue to this, with Malvolio appearing smiling, cross-gartered and in yellow stockings in Act III Scene 4, while Act IV Scene 2 finds Feste subjecting Malvolio to further torment in his own voice and more particularly in the voice of Sir Topas.

It will thus be seen that the basic contrasts are unifying elements in *Twelfth Night*, showing Shakespeare's keen sense of dramatic structure. And note that it is not just in scene and situation that this is done; it is also achieved by running associations. For example, Feste the fool is not a fool but an 'allowed

fool', Sir Andrew is a 'natural fool', while Olivia is guilty of folly;
almost everyone in the play, because of mistaken identity, is
'fooled' at one time or another, and this helps in the dove-tailing
of the main and subsidiary actions. Two of the chief binding
links are the Clown Feste and Maria, who can be equally at home
with Orsino or Olivia and with Sir Toby and his associates. Viola
too is an important link, for she is involved in the sub-plots; she
has a witty exchange with Feste, a brief but important one with
Malvolio when Olivia has sent the ring after her, and is caught
up in the duel with Sir Andrew, despite her appeals to Sir Toby
and Fabian. The student of *Twelfth Night* should look closely at
the integrated structure of the play. There are no loose ends, for
even Malvolio, though he leaves the stage bitterly, is going to be
entreated to 'a peace'.

## 2  *Mistaken identity*

The twin pivots of romance and comedy are served in *Twelfth
Night*, as in *The Two Gentlemen of Verona* and *As You Like It*, for
example, by the use of disguise, which in turn leads to mistaken
identity. The device of twins separated by shipwreck, each
believing the other dead, sets it all in motion. Viola's disguise as
Cesario deceives everyone, more particularly Orsino, who
employs Viola as a boy and confides in 'him'. Orsino's court is
taken in by Viola and, employed in a position of intimate trust by
Orsino, she compounds unwittingly that mistaken identity, for
Olivia, thinking her a man, falls in love with her. Already the
poignancy of her situation is being stressed, and it is deepened
when, thanks to the machinations of Sir Toby, aided and abetted
by Fabian, she finds herself forced into a duel with Sir Andrew.
And here the mistaken identity *motif* is given a subtle twist, for
not only is Viola represented as a man, she is represented as a
fearsome one to a man who is not a man and who is being
represented to her as fearsome too. Both are being given false
identities in the interests of the comedy, but the underlying
pathos of both their situations underpins the humour.

Viola is mistaken for Sebastian by Antonio as he is led in by
the officers and asks for the return of his purse; here again the
pathos of the situation is evident, but it gives Viola hope since
she hears Sebastian mentioned and believes that he is alive. The
priest further mistakes Viola for Sebastian, whom he has

betrothed to Olivia, so that the main effects of Viola's mistaken identity are seen to be romantic, pathetic, humorous and poignant. Sebastian is thought to be Viola/Cesario with conflicting results, but again the comic and romantic elements are markedly present.

At the beginning of Act IV the Clown Feste encounters Sebastian, mistakes him for Viola/Cesario (whom he had been sent to get for Olivia). Sebastian is bewildered but gives Feste money (as Viola had done before him) and, having been struck by Sir Andrew, retaliates in no uncertain manner. He is soon taken on by Sir Toby but, at a word from Olivia, the conspirators leave, their duel plans wrecked by Sebastian's aggression and Olivia's apprehensions on 'Cesario's' behalf. Thus the rough comedy gives way to romance, and Olivia leads away her lover, having mistaken him for the Cesario with whom she is in love. The delicacy of Viola's situation is neatly balanced by the real masculinity of Sebastian's; he fights, loves, is loyal, and the final revelation shows brother and sister as being markedly similar in appearance but extremely different in reactions. The only disquieting aspect of the mistaken identity role of Viola is seen when Duke Orsino reacts so violently to Olivia's love for 'Cesario' that he utters a threat which seems to be out of keeping with the spirit of the play:

But this, your minion, whom I know you love,
And whom, by heaven, I swear I tender dearly,
Him will I tear out of that cruel eye
Where he sits crowned in his master's spite.
(Act V Scene 1)

Of course he recants, but for one moment the romantic comedy teeters on the brink of potential tragedy. This demonstrates Shakespeare's variety in his handling of the main *motif* of the play.

This main *motif* is repeated on other levels and again subserves the principle of structural unity that was obviously present in Shakespeare's mind throughout *Twelfth Night*. Malvolio is twice fooled by believing what is not true; he mistakes the identity of the author of the letter counselling him to undertake eccentricities of fashion and to appear smiling. Maria has successfully counterfeited Olivia's handwriting, and Malvolio's error sets up the sub-plot which humiliates and degrades him. On the second occasion he mistakes the Clown's deliberately assumed voice of

'Sir Topas', and again it would seem that he *wants* to hear a voice outside those he knows have imprisoned him in darkness. The irony is implicit; Sir Topas the curate interrogates Malvolio the Puritan, yet there is no spiritual or religious identity for either.

## 3 Dramatic irony

Just as mistaken identity contributes to the unifying sense of structure, so dramatic irony is everywhere apparent and makes a like contribution in *Twelfth Night*. The basis of dramatic irony is the difference between the situation as known to the audience and as assumed by the characters of the play or by some of them. It will be quite obvious that it is intimately linked with mistaken identity, since from the outset the audience knows that Viola intends to assume masculine disguise. Every scene in which she appears, including much of the final scene, is therefore imbued with dramatic irony. In Act I Scene 4, for example, Viola's disguise as Cesario is undermined by her own aside at the end of the scene: 'yet, a barful strife!/Whoe'er I woo, myself would be his wife'. This tells the audience of her love, and this conscious-ness stresses the pathos of Viola's situation throughout the play. It is enhanced in the following scene where Viola courts Olivia in Orsino's name, affecting the speeches which she feels she ought to utter as a self-important man on an important 'embassy' which she hates!

Act III Scene 4 is perhaps the best example of dramatic irony in the Malvolio sub-plot, being succeeded by interaction with the main plot. Olivia sends for Malvolio because 'he is sad and civil', but he appears smiling, just as the audience knows he will according to the instructions of Maria's letter. Maria further suggests to Olivia that Malvolio is mad and, though we may dislike his overweening self-conceit, complacency and narrow-ness, we know that he is not. Here the dramatic irony produces a scene rich in comedy but with a somewhat sick overlay, since the plotters against Malvolio win the day by conveying him to the dark room.

There follows Sir Andrew's inept challenge to 'Cesario' and the duping of Viola into believing that she is to face an opponent who is, by Sir Toby's reportage, 'a devil in private brawl'. The irony is omnipresent, again inlaid with pathos, for example when Viola says 'I will return again into the house, and desire some conduct of the lady. I am no fighter.' But the scene is not yet finished, and Viola has to endure another kind of anxiety. The audience knows that she is not Sebastian, but Antonio can only believe his own eyes and is certain that she is. The result is poignant dramatic irony:

> This youth that you see here
> I snatch'd one half out of the jaws of death,
> Reliev'd him with such sanctity of love;
> And to his image, which methought did promise
> Most venerable worth, did I devotion.

Antonio's words move us and bewilder Viola; we know the truth, Viola doesn't. And this moment of dramatic irony provides even Sir Toby with fuel to re-ignite Sir Andrew's resolve, for he is able to observe of Viola 'A very dishonest paltry boy, and more a coward than a hare'. In *Twelfth Night* the effects of dramatic irony are cumulative, and it is the pivot on which the whole of the action in plot and sub-plots turns.

## Style

This general heading can in no way encompass the variety of Shakespeare's usage in *Twelfth Night*, and accordingly the various sub-headings given below should be studied for their selective detail and references.

### *Prose*

Approximately two-thirds of *Twelfth Night* is in prose. It is invariably used for the comic characters like Sir Toby, Feste the Clown and Sir Andrew, and for characters of a lower social position such as Maria, Fabian and Malvolio – though, as we shall see, the latter two speak in verse when the occasion demands. The use of prose was a literary convention of the time; the chief characters in plays – as in life – were kings and nobles, and they were given the elevated language of poetry in which to express themselves. Scenes in which the 'lower orders' of society appear are a contrast; these people were supposed to live on a lower plane of feeling than the main characters, and prose is therefore in perfect keeping with their modes of expression.

Letters and formal addresses were of course in prose, and the interested student will contrast the devious subtlety of Maria's letter, which combines verse (appropriate to Olivia's rank) and prose (appropriate to her 'lowering' herself to think of Malvolio in Act II Scene 5) with Malvolio's letter to Olivia in Act V Scene 1. Consider the inflated flourish of 'Some are born great, some achieve greatness, and some have greatness thrust upon 'em', which is calculated to heighten then prick Malvolio's vanity. Then note the direct and feeling expression of Malvolio's own prose after his humiliation: *Think of me as you please. I leave my duty a little unthought of, and speak out of my injury*', which has its own dignity. Or there is the sheer comedy of Sir Andrew's challenge to 'Cesario', 'Thy friend, as thou usest him, and thy sworn enemy', where the contradiction mirrors the simple confusion of Sir Toby's poor dupe.

The range of Shakespeare's prose in *Twelfth Night* is remarkable. There is Sir Toby's half-drunken 'A plague o' these pickleherrings! How now, sot?' as he enters belching to announce that Viola is at the gate. There is Feste's superb, never-at-a-loss running word-play in which he out-argues his superiors – sometimes for a tip – with the keen rationality of the professional fool who depends on words for his livelihood:

> Anything that's mended is but patched: virtue that transgresses is but patched with sin, and sin that amends is but patched with virtue. If that this simple syllogism will serve, so: if it will not, what remedy? As there is no true cuckold but calamity, so beauty's a flower. The lady bade take away the fool, therefore I say again, take her away. (Act I Scene 5)

Not only does the variety of prose contribute to our aesthetic pleasure, it also smacks of authenticity because it can naturally include contemporary references, which gives us the sense of real people living at a particular time, as in Fabian's 'you will hang like an icicle on a Dutchman's beard' and Maria's brilliant conceit on Malvolio, 'he does smile his face into more lines than is in the new map with the augmentation of the Indies'. This authenticity is also present in the dialogue, which is racy, meaningful, at times witty.

## Poetry

As we should expect in a romantic comedy, the poetry evocative of love is markedly present in the exchanges between Orsino and Viola and between Viola and Olivia. Again the variety in the blank verse line is remarkable in terms of mood, atmosphere, associations. In the first scene of the play that variety is displayed. There is the natural beauty of:

That strain again, it had a dying fall:
O, it came o'er my ear like the sweet sound
That breathes upon a bank of violets,
Stealing and giving odour.

This is balanced by affected conceits, like Orsino's comparison of himself to a hart (play on 'heart') in the self-indulgence of his own melancholy. There is Valentine's expression of Olivia's self-indulgence too, where she is said to 'water once a day her chamber round/With eye-offending brine', which is something of a parody of poetic as well as emotional excess. The dramatic irony referred to earlier is enhanced by lines of unconscious poetic truth, as when Orsino tells 'Cesario':

Diana's lip
Is not more smooth and rubious: thy small pipe
Is as the maiden's organ, shrill and sound,
And all is semblative a woman's part.
(Act I, Scene 5)

Indeed it is. Elsewhere we have quoted the beautiful 'Make me a willow cabin at your gate' speech of Viola, who pours her own love and romantic passion into words she could not otherwise express except here supposedly on Olivia's account. Just as Viola is at the thematic centre of *Twelfth Night*, so she is at the poetic centre too; here she defines her own situation with regard to Orsino, cleverly distancing it but making it poignant, indulging it but with the brave show of being separated from it:

she never told her love,
But let concealment like a worm i' th' bud
Feed on her damask cheek: she pin'd in thought,
And with a green and yellow melancholy
She sat like Patience on a monument,
Smiling at grief.
(Act II, Scene 4)

Rhyming couplets are used by Shakespeare to bring scenes to a close, but in *Twelfth Night* they are also used to heighten romantic expression. Olivia uses a rhyming couplet to persuade Sebastian to accompany her to their betrothal; Sebastian, to use Keats's phrase, 'poesied with hers in dewy rhyme', and he accepts in four rhyming lines. (Act IV, Scene 1).

It is a passage central to the plot and structure of *Twelfth Night*, reaching back into the play with its associations of the sea and the saving of Viola and Sebastian, the reference to 'boy' which is to be taken up by the Duke later in the same scene and applied to the same 'boy', Viola, while the 'love' and 'dedication' aptly describe Viola's loyalty and feeling for Orsino.

Shakespeare also employs broken lines to express strong feelings: consider Olivia's contemptuous rejection of any renewal of Orsino's suit. Admittedly, her feelings have perhaps been roused by 'Cesario's' failure to keep 'his' promise:

If it be aught to the old tune, my lord,
It is as fat as fulsome to mine ear
As howling after music. (Act V Scene 1)

The expression in a play which has some affectations is commendably blunt here, the unconsciously ironic reference to music, so treasured by Orsino in his melancholy, perhaps provoking the anger of his reply. Two other instances of poetic usage may be referred to here. Malvolio, who normally speaks in prose, has his expression of ill-usage raised into verse (in V,1). It is a fitting and cunning stroke on Shakespeare's part, giving dignity to a character who has been subjected to indignity, and thus perhaps indicating some sympathy for him. This, followed by Olivia's compassionate response, moves Fabian to revelation and confession, also in verse. The variety of verse has only been touched on here; it can be elevated, conversational, in couplets, parody, romantic, angry, bitter, or any variant of these. Its variety, like Cleopatra's, is infinite.

### Word-play

*Twelfth Night* is rich in word-play, ranging from a succession of puns, which begin with Orsino's 'hart' sequence in the first scene where that word is used twice, followed by 'heart' some dozen lines later. Viola, even in her grief, half-puns on 'Illyria' and 'Elysium', while she and the Captain play on the word 'perchance' as well. This sets the pattern for the punning and quibbling which runs the length of the play, the tipsy Sir Toby taking up Maria's 'confine' and following that with a play on 'tall' in description of Sir Andrew. 'Nature' provides the lead into Maria's punning on the word 'natural'; and so it goes on. The

majority of puns are listed in the textual notes, and it is notice-
able that this form of word-play is another strand of unity
between the main and the sub-plots. But one character, Feste,
lives by words alone; he earns his livelihood by his adept usages
and, as we have seen, sometimes gains tips when the ingenuity
he shows is appreciated by others. He raises word-play to a fine
art; invents learned-sounding words and reverts to prover-
bialisms like *cucullus non facit monachum* in order to prove his
verbal arguments (Act I, Scene 5).

## Soliloquies and asides

Both of these are employed here, and once again it is Viola and
the poignancy of her situation that calls forth the revealing *aside*
to the audience, and the longer pondering on her feelings,
which constitutes *soliloquy*. There is little room in the sub-plots
for these, since the action, whether contemplated or immediate,
is of paramount importance. Viola, on the other hand, has brief
periods in which to comment on or review her position. Thus at
the end of Act I, Scene 4 she vows to do her best for Orsino in
his suit to Olivia, but tells the audience that she herself loves
him, thus enhancing the dramatic irony of the coming exchanges with Olivia and Orsino. This is complemented at the
end of the next scene where Olivia is twice left alone and reveals
her own love at first sight for Viola/Cesario – 'Even so quickly
may one catch the plague?'

This aspect of the main plot now moves quickly; Malvolio
'returns' Olivia's ring to Viola, and the latter, in a moving soliloquy of some twenty-four lines, ponders on the effect of her
disguise and concludes, rightly, 'She loves me, sure' (Act II,
Scene 2). Other instances of Viola's soliloquizing are her sympathetic appraisal of Feste after she has held her own with him
in verbal argument (Act III, Scene 1) and her pondering on
Antonio's words about Sebastian. Her soliloquies are complemented by Olivia's asides as she contemplates her own love for
Viola/Cesario ('O what a deal of scorn looks beautiful/In the
contempt and anger of his lip') before turning to 'him' and
confessing it openly (Act III, Scene 1), or her aside in Act III,
Scene 4 where she says that she has sent for 'Cesario' and, as
prelude to that meeting, asks for Malvolio – 'He is sad and civil' –
as appropriate to her own mood.

Sebastian also has a soliloquy after his bewildering encounter with Olivia, ponders on the whereabouts of Antonio, and considers that either he or Olivia, or both of them, must be mad. This device is of course more common in the tragedies, where characters have serious thoughts or motives (like Macbeth and Othello) or dilemmas of decision (like Hamlet) or crises of consequences (like Lear).

But *Twelfth Night* has one soliloquy which has the interaction not only of the audience but watchers on stage, and here one feels that Shakespeare has perfected and extended the basic device. We refer, of course, to the box-tree scene of Act II Scene 5. Here Malvolio is only *apparently* alone, so that his musings and vanity-filled words are overheard by Sir Toby, Fabian and Sir Andrew hidden in the box-tree. So self-absorbed is Malvolio that he has no knowledge of their presence and does not hear their remarks. The result, as Malvolio talks on 'alone', is fast and farcical humour.

### Song

Orsino's interest in music as echoing his mood in *Twelfth Night* is complemented by the actual songs in the play, each of which fits neatly into the mood, structure and atmosphere. The first one, 'O Mistress mine' is sung by the Clown Feste in Act II Scene 3. The general theme is 'love now while you can, don't delay' but its tone is poignant and it appears to radiate out into the play, for 'journeys end in lovers meeting' is a forecast of the final coming together of the lovers in Act V, Scene 1.

The final song of the play comments on the various phases of life from childhood to age, and though its texture has been criticized it is in many ways a fitting conclusion. It looks back at the career of Sir Toby (though of course without mentioning him), what one critic has referred to as the 'Drunkard's Progress', but it has a general philosophical content. Its tone is to express the way life is, as contrasted with the main action of the play, which is how life isn't – sentimentalized, romanticized, illusory. Life is rain; the play is festive sunshine but has, if you like, its showers of melancholy and its sordidness (witness Sir Toby's behaviour). Thus at particular points in the play a song is used as commentary on situations central to it, with the last song a comment as well on life itself.

# Imagery

The images used in *Twelfth Night* cover a wide range but no particular sequence dominates. As befits a play with a shipwreck involving the central characters, there are images of the sea, of music, of nature, and a number of classical references. For example, the sea captain tells Viola that he saw Sebastian struggling 'like Arion on the dolphin's back' (Act I, Scene 2), and Orsino says of Viola 'Diana's lip/Is not more smooth and rubious' in his belief – ironically – that Viola will influence Olivia into returning his (Orsino's) love. Viola uses clichéd images in order to emphasize that love (or perhaps cunningly to undermine it by stressing its excess), like 'With groans that thunder love, with sighs of fire'. Even the 'willow cabin' poetry – the willow being the symbol of melancholy love – continues to stress an extreme of emotion or simulated emotion. Viola's own emotion is, however, real and she uses both natural and abstract imagery to express it; note the fine focus conveyed by such phrases as

> she never told her love,
> But let concealment like a worm i' th' bud
> Feed on her damask cheek: (Act II, Scene 4)

Here her own 'concealment' and the effect it is having on her is being obliquely expressed through the imagery. She follows it with 'She sat like Patience on a monument/Smiling at grief', an abstraction in which she tries to move away (in order to avoid suspicion) from her own case by using a visual personification.

The comedy of the box-tree scene is heightened by the force of the hunting images used by Sir Toby and Fabian ('He is now at a cold scent . . . Sowter will cry upon't for all this, though it be as rank as a fox') to describe Malvolio's responses to Maria's letter. Maria herself speaks of Malvolio in a simile that mocks his appearance when she says that he is 'like a pedant that keeps a school i' th' church', while Antonio describes his desire to follow Sebastian in case he encounters danger as 'More sharp than filed steel'. Sir Toby uses contemporary images ('scout me for him at the corner of the orchard, like a bum-baily') and in anticipation of the Viola/Sir Andrew duel, 'they will kill one another by the look, like cockatrices'. The examples given above are a selection from the rich variety of imagery used in *Twelfth Night*.

## Atmosphere

The title of the play allies it with festivity and revelry – a performance for 'Twelfth Night' – and it is, despite aspects of the Malvolio
scenes, the sunniest and most harmonious of Shakespeare's comedies  The nature of the humour has been examined under the
various headings of this section, under the individual characters,
and also glossed in the textual notes. Hazlitt wrote that it was
'perhaps too good-natured for comedy' and remarked that it had
'little satire, and no spleen. It aims at the ludicrous rather than the
ridiculous. It makes us laugh at the follies of mankind, not despise
them, and still less bear any ill-will towards them.'

Situations are viewed without sentiment, contempt, or satire;
Shakespeare has a keen eye for all absurdities, for genuine comic
figures and situations. Although wit and a variety of humour are
the dominant notes, there is a partly serious background, which
throws the comedy into relief. Olivia has just had a double
bereavement; Viola and Sebastian each think the other has been
drowned; life holds nothing for Orsino while Olivia's doors are
shut against him. Viola faces (supposedly) a duel, perhaps death,
and cannot make known her love; Olivia loves a dream; Antonio
is arrested and doesn't know his fate. And the sane Malvolio is
imprisoned as a madman by those whose *raison d'être* is practical
joking. But all these are set against fun and ultimate happiness
(except for Malvolio). The grip on character, as we have seen,
enhances the picture of human life in the play. Buffoonery runs
alongside wit; there are the scenes of carousal, the garden scene
where Malvolio is 'practising behaviour to his own shadow'. In the
mock duel the atmosphere is conveyed by the action – and *Twelfth
Night* is essentially a play of action. This action is complemented
by dialogue, as we have seen, with its wit, puns, abuse and misuse
of words and dexterity in argument or idiocy in repetition as we
see in Feste and Sir Andrew respectively. All these contribute to
the festive atmosphere of *Twelfth Night*.

## Themes

These are intimately bound up with *Atmosphere*, for the serious
and humorous parts of the play are unified by contrasting or
common treatment. There is the theme of *sentimental love*
(Orsino–Olivia) and of *true love* (Viola); in the sub-plots this is

*self-love* (Malvolio) and perhaps even a comic mirroring of true love (Sir Toby and Maria). The theme of *natural perfection* (Viola) is offset against the imperfections of Orsino and Olivia (*melancholy self-indulgence*), Malvolio (*vanity and pride*) and Sir Toby (*irresponsible jesting*).

Linked with these of course is the theme of *self-deception* which goes right across the play from Orsino through Malvolio to Sir Andrew. Ultimately the themes fuse at the end of the play into expressions of reunion (Viola and Sebastian), self-discovery (Olivia and Orsino) and possibly of reconciliation, if Malvolio can be entreated 'to a peace'. It must be stressed that the thematic content of *Twelfth Night* exists only in its action; to give it a strong moral or philosophical weighting would be to distort the nature of the play.

# Further reading

*Twelfth Night: The Arden Shakespeare*. edited by J. M. Lothian and T. W Craik (Methuen, 1975). (See particularly xxxv– xcviii.)

*The First Night of 'Twelfth Night'*, Leslie Hotson (London 1954).

*Twelfth Night*, Barbara Hardy (Basil Blackwell, 1963).

*Twentieth Century Interpretations of 'Twelfth Night'*. Edited by Walter King (Prentice Hall, New Jersey, 1968).

*'Twelfth Night' and Shakespearean Comedy*, Clifford Leech (1965).

*Shakespeare and his Comedies*, John Russell Brown (London 1957).

*Shakespeare's Festive Comedy*, C. L. Barber (Princeton, 1959).

# Pan study aids Selected titles published in the Brodie's Notes Series

**Thomas Mann** Death in Venice  Tonio Kröger

**Christopher Marlowe** Doctor Faustus  Edward the Second

**W. Somerset Maugham** Of Human Bondage

**Thomas Middleton** The Changeling

**Arthur Miller** The Crucible  Death of a Salesman

**John Milton** A Choice of Milton's Verse  Comus and Samson Agonistes
Paradise Lost I, II

**Bill Naughton** Spring and Port Wine

**R. O'Brien** Z for Zachariah

**Sean O'Casey** Juno and the Paycock
The Shadow of a Gunman and the Plough and the Stars

**George Orwell** Animal Farm  1984

**Alexander Pope** Selected Poetry

**J. B. Priestley** An Inspector Calls

**J. D. Salinger** The Catcher in the Rye

**Siegfried Sassoon** Memoirs of a Fox-Hunting Man

**William Shakespeare** Antony and Cleopatra  As You Like It  Coriolanus
Hamlet  Henry IV (Part I)  Henry IV (Part II)  Henry V  Julius Caesar  King Lear
Love's Labour's Lost  Macbeth  Measure for Measure  The Merchant of Venice
A Midsummer Night's Dream  Much Ado about Nothing  Othello  Richard II
Richard III  Romeo and Juliet  The Sonnets  The Taming of the Shrew  The Tempest
Twelfth Night  The Winter's Tale

**G. B. Shaw** Pygmalion  Saint Joan

**John Steinbeck** The Grapes of Wrath  Of Mice and Men  The Pearl

**Tom Stoppard** Rosencrantz and Guildenstern are Dead

**Jonathan Swift** Gulliver's Travels

**Dylan Thomas** Under Milk Wood

**Mark Twain** Huckleberry Finn

**H. G. Wells** The History of Mr Polly  The War of the Worlds

**Oscar Wilde** The Importance of Being Earnest

**William Wordsworth** The Prelude (Books 1, 2)

**W. B. Yeats** Selected Poetry

**GCSE English coursework:** Prose G. Handley and P. Wilkins

**GCSE English coursework:** Drama and Poetry K. Dowling